BEYOND THE RAPIST

Beyond the Rapist

Title IX and Sexual Violence on US Campuses

Kate Lockwood Harris

OXFORD
UNIVERSITY PRESS

OXFORD
UNIVERSITY PRESS

Oxford University Press is a department of the University of Oxford. It furthers
the University's objective of excellence in research, scholarship, and education
by publishing worldwide. Oxford is a registered trade mark of Oxford University
Press in the UK and certain other countries.

Published in the United States of America by Oxford University Press
198 Madison Avenue, New York, NY 10016, United States of America.

© Oxford University Press 2019

Library of Congress Cataloging-in-Publication Data
Names: Harris, Kate Lockwood, author.
Title: Beyond the rapist : title IX and Sexual Violence on US Campuses
university sexual violence / Kate Lockwood Harris.
Description: New York : Oxford University Press, 2019. | Includes
bibliographical references and index.
Identifiers: LCCN 2018038472 (print) | LCCN 2018055742 (ebook) |
ISBN 9780190876944 (updf) | ISBN 9780190876951 (epub) |
ISBN 9780190876968 (online content) | ISBN 9780190876937 (paperback) |
ISBN 9780190876920 (cloth)
Subjects: LCSH: Rape in universities and colleges—United States—Prevention. |
Sexual harassment in universities and colleges—United States—Prevention. |
BISAC: COMPUTERS / General. | LANGUAGE ARTS & DISCIPLINES /
Communication Studies. | SOCIAL SCIENCE / General.
Classification: LCC LB2345.3.R37 (ebook) |
LCC LB2345.3.R37 H36 2019 (print) | DDC 371.7/82—dc23
LC record available at https://lccn.loc.gov/2018038472

9 8 7 6 5 4 3 2 1

Paperback Printed by WebCom, Inc., Canada
Hardback Printed by Bridgeport National Bindery, Inc., United States of America

Contents

Acknowledgments

To everyone who has supported, provoked, encouraged, read, reviewed, criticized, and engaged with this book at each stage of its development: Thank you.

To my peers, friends, and colleagues: Thank you. My gratitude extends especially to Jason Barry, Sarah Blithe, Elizabeth Eger, Kristen Foht, James Fortney, Jenna Hanchey, Tim Huffman, Shawna Malvini Redden, Jamie McDonald, Kristina Ruiz-Mesa, and Amy Way.

To my teachers and mentors: Thank you. You each challenged me to pursue this project. You gave your smarts and your time. That generosity made this project possible, though the faults in the pages that follow are all mine. I am especially thankful for Karen Ashcraft, Natalie Fixmer-Oraiz, Lisa Flores, Deepti Misri, Pete Simonson, Bryan Taylor, and Julia Wood.

To the institutions that sustained this work, especially the libraries, parks, and museums I haunted while writing: Thank you.

To all of you who have offered me love or received mine: Thank you.

To my fellow dancers: Thank you.

To all of you who have survived and/or fought against sexual violence: Thank you. I am grateful for your anger, grief, compassion, and creativity.

To scholars and students who are earlier in their careers and studies than I am: Thank you for your curiosity, wisdom, and conviction. I hope this writing invites you to continue learning from and contributing to the field. I hope you find in it the space to call out and call in what is missing in and problematic about this book and the academy.

Why "beyond the rapist"?

When I began research for this book, the U.S. Department of Education was investigating three universities for mishandling sexual assaults on campus. In the intervening years, the number of institutions under investigation for violations of Title IX grew to 225 by January 2017. In a country where approximately one in five college women and more than half of lesbian, gay, bisexual, transgender, and queer (LGBTQ) students experience sexual assault, many colleges are under intense scrutiny as they work to better prevent and address violence. This book project takes up this social problem—how organizations respond to sexual violence—and considers it in relation to a persistent theoretical dilemma in my academic subfield, organizational communication: How are organization and violence related, and what does that relationship have to do with communication? The book illustrates how feminist new materialism and communication theory offer insights about the problem of rape on U.S. campuses. It looks "beyond the rapist" to consider how complex physical and symbolic components of violence are embedded in organizations.

The increase in federal investigations is one result of activism across the United States. Students and recent graduates have developed a network to educate the public, support survivors of sexual violence, and assert their right to education without assault. The changes these groups advocate are hard won. I asked a prominent member of this network, a woman who filed a federal complaint against her university after she was raped, to describe what it was like trying to hold her school accountable to federal law. She mentioned that the Office for Civil Rights investigates complaints, but, in the meantime, her school continues to violate her rights. For her, justice seems slow if not altogether elusive. Indeed in 2014, the average length of an investigation was more than 4 years (New, 2015). Describing her progress toward graduation she said, "I've had to take years off my education. I want more than anything else to move on with my life, put this behind me. . . . I didn't sign up to sacrifice my life and education for the well-being of an institution." Like many people at the heart of the movement to change campus sexual violence, she has had first-hand encounters with institutional inertia and inappropriate university responses: She was banned from campus because of a mental health issue common among rape survivors, but her assailant was not sanctioned at all. As she and so many others point out, the impact of sexual violence does not stop the moment a rapist ends an assault on one person's body.

Yet among the general public, the label "violence" is often applied solely to moments of physical injury. As the above survivor's comments illustrate, this common understanding of violence is not sufficiently nuanced to address the complex systems that shape what happens on college campuses. In the arguments that follow, I apply insights from feminist new materialism in order to recognize organizational forms of violence. In so doing, I refute the idea that a violent actor is always an individual human. Instead, I trace the ways in which universities participate in violent processes. Furthermore, by considering violent aspects of communication, I detail complex relationships between symbolic and physical systems. Throughout, I adopt an intersectional approach (Crenshaw, 1991). It weaves together gender, race, and sexuality to demonstrate how sexual violence is a symptom of persistent institutional inequities.

Those inequities are sustained—in part—through communication. This word, "communication," often signals mere talk or words, but I use it in a slightly different sense. Many scholars of communication have noted that our field focuses on symbols but does not always adequately explain how those symbols are related to material objects and physical forces (e.g., Ashcraft & Harris, 2014). Some of these scholars have suggested that my discipline—communication studies—should make a "material turn," that it should better account for material and physical phenomena (Hallenbeck, 2012; Robichaud & Cooren, 2013). As the book proceeds, I advance that material turn by considering violence, and specifically sexual violence, in relationship to emerging theory. I trace the components of assault that both precede and exceed a moment of rape such that sexual violence can be understood as a continuously organized, material–discursive phenomenon. The concept "violence" provides a concrete illustration of why it matters for communication scholars to theorize the physical world with nuance.

My engagement with the material turn is not a wholesale endorsement, as emerging theory risks diminishing the power of symbols to change the world. Accordingly, I invite communication scholars to pay closer attention to power and difference as the field makes this turn toward the material. On many campuses, and for the public at large, questions remain about the extent to which sexual assault occurs, and sometimes people doubt that it occurs at all. Though experts have consensus about the prevalence of rape and related instances of sexist–racist–homophobic discrimination, many people still want proof of the problem. Yet this kind of "proof" depends upon a set of ideas that disconnect physical and symbolic violence and thus make it difficult to document a troubling problem in terms that dominant groups accept.

Furthermore, organizations have often discounted the strength of discourse in order to preserve the status quo. Accordingly, even as I show how a material turn can be useful for responding differently to campus sexual violence, I want to preserve some of the power of symbols.

Why "beyond the rapist"?

Many feminists—and particularly feminists of color—argue that to eradicate rape, society must begin to look beyond the rapist (e.g., Chen, Dulani, & Piepzna-Samarasinha, 2016; INCITE!, 2016; Sokoloff, 2005). They suggest that individual rapists should be held accountable for their violence, but that merely punishing perpetrators misses something crucially important: the links between interpersonal violence and broader systems of oppression. When organizations focus primarily on single acts of violence, they can constantly defer real transformation and need not dismantle broader oppressive systems. Indeed, far from undoing oppression, organizations often reinforce those existing systems of injustice, even as they work to address individual instances of sexual violence.

In this book, I use the term "sexual violence" to reference ongoing sexism and racism that manifests not only during assault but also in organizational processes. I think along with scholars such as Smith (2005) who argued that "sexual violence is a tool by which certain peoples become marked as inherently 'rapable.' These peoples then are violated, not only through direct sexual assault, but through a wide variety of state policies, ranging from environmental racism to sterilization abuse" (p. 3). Smith's definition of sexual violence encompasses single assaults and also includes broader processes of bodily harm. Yet prevailing understandings of sexual violence rely on atomistic frameworks. For instance, people who combat rape via the law encounter the "judicial preference for the individualist model" (Messer-Davidow, 2002, p. 275). The law sees assaults as separate and distinct, not as a pattern. Moreover, the justice system has often reinforced racial stereotypes that associate blackness with violent hypersexuality (Bumiller, 2008). As A. Davis (2000) argued succinctly, "because the primary strategies for addressing violence against women rely on the state and on constructing gendered assaults on women as 'crimes,' the criminalization process further bolsters the racism of the courts and prisons. Those institutions, in turn, further contribute to violence against women" (para. 15). When sexual violence is conceptualized as an individual event rather than a collective social process, society can overlook the unequal systems and structures that sexual violence enacts (Hengehold, 2000; Mohanty, 2003). To create a more robust transformation of the large-scale structures that enable rape, we must look beyond—but not over—the rapist. To focus merely on individual perpetrators blunts effective critique of sexism, racism, homophobia, and other axes upon which unequal power is conferred upon social groups.

Overview and history of Title IX

Even though the U.S. justice system most readily recognizes individual crimes, the movement transforming university responses to sexual violence has relied upon this system. A number of groups have successfully used Title IX and related federal laws to agitate for organizational reform and transformation.

Title IX came into law in 1972 as part of the federal Education Amendments. It was developed in close relationship with other key civil rights protections, including antidiscrimination measures on the basis of race and national origin. Indeed, an early draft of the legislation proposed amending Title VI of the Civil Rights Act in order to ban discrimination not only on the basis of race, but also on the basis of sex/gender. Ultimately, legislators did not take that path forward and instead developed an independent statute. By 1975, the U.S. Department of Health, Education, and Welfare had detailed specific regulations under Title IX, and President Gerald Ford signed them. Some of those early regulations are similar to the requirements colleges and universities must meet today. They specify that campuses must have a designated Title IX officer and that students must receive information about how to file a complaint if they experience discrimination.

Title IX bars gender discrimination in educational programs that receive federal support. It states, "No person in the United States shall, on the basis of sex, be excluded from participation in, be denied the benefits of, or be subject to discrimination under any educational programs or activity receiving federal financial assistance" (Title IX of the Education Amendments of 1972). Sometimes people think Title IX applies only to college athletics, but it actually bars sex discrimination in varied aspects of higher education, including but not limited to career education, access to college, the learning environment, standardized testing, and technology utilization. It further provides protections for pregnant and parenting students.

In the early 1990s a key case set the groundwork for much of today's activism on sexual violence. A U.S. Supreme Court ruling established that individuals who experienced sex/gender discrimination can sue their colleges or universities for financial compensation (*Franklin v. Gwinnet County Public Schools*, 1992). The same case established that a university can be held responsible for the discriminatory actions of one of its members.

After that, the first highly publicized case regarding sexual assault and Title IX occurred when Lisa Simpson and Anne

Gilmore sued the University of Colorado in the early 2000s (*Simpson v. University of Colorado*, 2005; 2007). Members of the university's football team, as well as recruits, raped Simpson. The case hinged on whether the university had been "deliberately indifferent" regarding the risk of sexual assault. After the trial court found in favor of the university, an appeals court overruled the decision. The appeals court stated that the university had plenty of knowledge of behaviors likely to lead to sexual assault and, furthermore, encouraged those behaviors. The court also cited the university's knowledge of earlier incidents as evidence that it was deliberately indifferent. Several years prior to Simpson's assault, a few women reported that football team members had assaulted them. Among them was female football team member Katie Hnida, who was raped by another football player. The Simpson case led to what is still one of the largest payouts to Title IX complainants: $2.5 million to Simpson, $350,000 to Gilmore.

After that case was settled in 2007, more students started to bring federal complaints against their schools through the Office for Civil Rights. Some of the most publicly visible cases happened at the University of North Carolina at Chapel Hill, where Andrea Pino, Annie E. Clark, and Landen Gambill all made national headlines for fighting the university's mishandling of sexual assault. At the same time, the public became increasingly aware of rape on college campuses. Both the 2015 documentary *The Hunting Ground* and Jon Krakauer's 2015 book *Missoula: Rape and the Justice System in a College Town* heightened visibility of the problem. Amid increasing scrutiny, and given the savvy of activists across the country, the number of schools under federal investigation grew by a dramatic 6,600% between 2010 and the end of 2015.

As of 2017, Title IX worked alongside several other laws that also govern U.S. universities' response to sexual violence. The

Clery Act of 1990 requires universities to send mass notifications when campus security is at risk. It also obligates colleges to publish annual statistics about crimes on campus. In 2013, the Violence Against Women Act was renewed and included the Campus Sexual Violence Act provision. That part of the law clarified or reinforced some existing requirements and added new ones. For instance, though the Clery Act already required universities to track and report incidents of sexual assault, the renewal of the Violence Against Women Act required universities also to track and report stalking and dating violence. To provide guidance about these complex laws, the U.S. Department of Education issued several statements, including multiple "Dear Colleague" letters, that clarify schools' obligations to prevent, educate about, and respond to sexual violence.

Like all social movements, the one organized around Title IX and related laws has both successes and weaknesses. Though many individuals involved in the movement are attentive to the dynamics of racism, cisnormativity, and homophobia, the survivors who are most publicly recognizable tend to be white, heterosexual, U.S. citizen women. The racism and nationalism that enshrouds these identities may, paradoxically, help the movement gain traction. For example, in a case against Florida State settled in 2016, the university paid $950,000 to Erica Kinsman, a white woman. Jameis Winston, a black man, and the quarterback of the school's football team, raped Kinsman in 2012. After the university mishandled its response to her case, Kinsman filed a Title IX complaint with the Office for Civil Rights and a lawsuit against the school. Title IX was an important mechanism that held both Winston and Florida State accountable for wrongdoing. Even so, efforts to combat sexual violence—particularly its institutional dynamics—can reference and even reinforce stereotypes of hypersexual black men and gloss the country's long history of deploying racism in order to protect white womanhood (Enck-Wanzer, 2009). This book is implicated in some of the same problematic paradoxes that have helped the movement against campus sexual violence to garner national attention. Because it focuses on colleges, the book centers the experiences and processes of people who are relatively privileged within the United States. Higher education remains exclusive: As of 2015, only 33% of adults in the United States held a bachelor's degree (Ryan & Bauman, 2016), and the majority of students who enter college in the United States are white (National Center for Education Statistics, n.d.). These power dynamics play a role in the movement's visibility and also in the availability of a market for a book like this one.

Given the complexities surrounding Title IX's history, implementation, and public traction, how can schools begin to think "beyond the rapist" to dismantle the systems that support rape? An emerging intellectual tradition with roots in decades of intellectual and activist work—one called feminist new materialism—provides some starting points.

Feminist new materialism

Feminist new materialism is a set of intellectual, political, and ethical assumptions. Feminist new materialists couple matter with meaning, the natural with the cultural, the physical with the symbolic. Scholars who advance this thinking tend to conceptualize these aspects of existence as intertwined or "intra-acting" (Barad, 2007) rather than bifurcated. In this view, people do not find words to name and describe a table that already exists. Nor do people's names and descriptions create the idea of the table and allow people to experience it. Instead, the table and the descriptions of it simultaneously co-constitute each other. Neither operates independently.

Feminist new materialism has emerged, in part, from a growing dissatisfaction with tenets of social construction. Charging that scholars have overused the symbolic and the discursive as explanations for social phenomena, a number of academics suggest "language has been granted too much power" (Barad, 2003, p. 801). In one version of this critique, Reed (2000) charged that radical social construction "tends to idealize meaning and to marginalize the non-semantic aspects of economic and political reality . . . it is ontologically insensitive to material structuring and its constraining influence on social action" (p. 525). Often, though not always, critiques like these are motivated by political concerns. Speaking of global climate change, Latour (2004) observed:

> the danger . . . no longer [comes] from an excessive confidence in ideological arguments posturing as matters of fact—as we have learned to combat so efficiently in the past—but from an excessive *distrust* of good matters of fact disguised as bad ideological biases! While we spent years trying to detect the real prejudices hidden behind the appearance of objective statements, do we now have to reveal the real objective and incontrovertible facts hidden behind the *illusion* of prejudices? . . . Extremists are using the very same argument of social construction to destroy hard-won evidence that could save our lives. (p. 227)

As a number of intellectuals argue, our ability to assert the real— to uphold the material and physical facts of the world—seems to have slipped. If we cannot account for facts, we cannot make changes needed to bring about a more just world. And yet, even as it resonates with some of these critiques, feminist new materialism takes a different starting point, one that refuses to reinforce the division between material and symbol.

The "materialism" in feminist new materialism refers neither to the historical materialism of Marxism nor to the excessive consumption in Madonna's "Material Girl." Instead, "material" refers variously to bodies, to objects, to texts, and even, as I outline in the next chapter, to discourse. Because physical and symbolic worlds "intra-act," scholars working from this tradition assume that objects can act upon the world. No longer is agency—the ability to have influence—the sole province of humans (or even animals). Instead, the world includes myriad actors, human and nonhuman alike.

Feminist new materialism both asserts the real and challenges claims about reality (van der Tuin, 2009), and it does so with political aims in mind. To abandon social construction altogether would be detrimental to efforts to establish gender–racial equality. Indeed, the idea that gender is learned—not innate—predicates much of feminist activism. By contrast, to abandon physical explanations of gender—the notion of biological difference as well as the embodied experience of gender—would also put feminist projects in peril. Claims that society is "beyond" or "post" gender, or that inequality no longer exists, abound in a world intent on dampening feminism's capacity to invoke a more just social life. I detail the distinctive ways in which feminist new materialism intervenes in these dynamics in the next chapter.

What's new about feminist new materialism?

The "new" in "feminist new materialism" should not be read literally. The word usually denotes something that did not exist before, but to interpret it as such in this context would be to miss something important. Feminist new materialism is not new in the usual sense of the word, but it is not identical to prior feminist materialisms. Barad (2014) said directly, "There is nothing that is new; there is nothing that is not new" (p. 168). These seemingly paradoxical claims emerge from feminist new materialism's somewhat counterintuitive approach to time, one that situates feminist new materialism's distinctiveness in deep relationship with feminist pasts and futures.

Feminists have long been suspicious of progress narratives and the idea of an inevitably more just and equitable future (e.g., Fannin, MacLeavy, Larner, & Wang, 2014; Scott, 1997). Grosz (2010) even described feminist theory as "untimely" (p. 49). Feminists often reject linear accounts of history and understand time to be continuously overlapping. The "wave" metaphor used to characterize crests in activism across decades is one example of this cyclical orientation. Articulating this stance, Minh-ha (1989) said, "Every gesture, every word involves our past, present, and future" (p. 122). Given this understanding of time as concurrent, feminist new materialists consistently note that their thinking is "not a defensive break with a feminist past" but a feminist habit that "renders its texts and its practices wholly relevant to a feminist present and future" (Hinton & van der Tuin, 2014, p. 3). A similar genealogy is available in varied academic disciplines. For example, the seeds of feminist "new" materialism exist in the last five decades of feminist communication scholarship (K. L. Harris, 2016a). This orientation to history enables relational maintenance across generations, a feature typical of feminist new materialist accounts of intellectual archives.

Feminists tell these careful, interested histories to intervene in intellectual power dynamics. The politics of citation catapult a few individuals—who are usually white, male, and European or U.S. American—to academic popstar status (see, e.g., Chakravartty, Kuo, Grubbs, & McIlwain, 2018). Meanwhile, those scholars writing their songs—usually somehow Other— are forgotten or barred from the performance stage. Wiegman

(1995) detailed this dynamic. She noticed that, in accounts of feminisms, intersectionality is frequently spoken of as a remedy for earlier feminisms. This story falsely positions feminisms of color as a derivative of white feminism. Exacerbating this pattern of false and incomplete origins, scholars and publics continue to think—mistakenly—that writing emanates from a single author whose brilliance is divorced from community. Amid the persistent fiction and fetishizing of independent authorship, feminist new materialism's nonlinear time challenges some of the problematic, territorializing practices that organize the academy (Dolphijn & van der Tuin, 2012).

Like any stories about where we have been, where we are now, and where we are going, feminist new materialism's interventions in the political dynamics of intellectual history do not escape those politics: Clare (2016) suggested that feminist new materialism underemphasizes its relationship to feminist Marxisms, and numerous scholars argue that feminist new materialism poorly accounts for its imbrication with decolonial and antiracist scholarship or even replicates colonialism and racism (Ahmed, 2008; Irni, 2013; Todd, 2016).

On the whole, feminist new materialism is "rethinking the nature of epistemic shifts" (van der Tuin, 2011, p. 271). As I detail in the next chapter, it continues feminism's complex work on the relationship between sex and gender by challenging a pervasive mode of thought that separates materiality (which is sometimes conflated with nature) from discourse (which is sometimes conflated with culture). Importantly, feminist new materialism rethinks these relationships by problematizing distinctions between "human" and "nonhuman," thereby wresting the capacity to act from anthropocentric intention. This style of academic work, of drawing upon feminist histories in present contexts, proceeds via "transposition" (Braidotti, 2006) whereby a melodic passage is translated to a higher or lower register. Its relation to a previous iteration is recognizable, but the altered passage is distinct. I trace these distinct aspects of the theory in more detail in the next chapter.

Feminist new materialism and sexual violence

Feminist new materialists often argue that materiality is undertheorized, underexplained, or altogether absent, but the theoretical trouble with violence is somewhat different: When publics discuss violence, sometimes all they notice is the physical, embodied, material manifestations of violence. When sexual violence occurs, the seeming absence of "hard" evidence— bruises, blood, and torn flesh—leads some people to conclude rape did not actually occur. Moreover, a focus on overly physical understandings of sexual violence lets publics think only about individual perpetrators who rape and ignore or overlook all the ways in which culture supports, legitimizes, and sets up the conditions for rapists to commit violence with impunity. Feminist new materialist thinking is useful for theorizing and analyzing violence not because it turns attention more fully to the physical and material, but because it refuses to separate the material from the discursive. It can help illustrate how rape is organized via material–discursive intra-actions. Moreover, though the rapist never drops from view, it locates the problem of sexual violence beyond the rapist, in systems rather than individuals.

Communication and sexual violence

Many of us have heard the children's schoolyard saying, "Sticks and stones can break my bones but words can never hurt me." In this commonplace, words and symbols cannot do harm. When we discuss this phrase in the classes I teach, my students often assert the importance of having a "thick skin." I agree with them that skills for deflecting verbal jabs are necessary. But this aphorism is also problematic because it suggests that violence is only physical. To accept its framework means missing important ways in which symbols and language support inequity on the basis of difference. Its premise cannot explain how hate speech participates in the violence of white supremacy, nor can it explain how verbal abuse and beatings work together during intimate partner violence.

On the other hand, if my students and I lapse into the realm of fantasy, we encounter similar problems with understanding violence. In the fantastical world of Harry Potter, Severus Snape is able to slice off an ear by uttering mere words. Voldemort uses language to make people writhe in physical pain. In this imaginary world, words and violence collapse. The distance between saying and slaying disappears. This iteration of the violence–communication relationship, too, is a problem. In it, we miss opportunities to understand moments when communication enacts nonviolence and when communication can intervene in violence. Whether communication and violence are wholly separate or the same, in either extreme rendering we lose the ability to distinguish more and less violent speech. Together, these two positions allow society to see norms of civility as nonviolent, even when they are used to halt marginalized groups' demands that "civil," dominant groups end their violence.

Neither of these positions—the one associated with common sense, the one associated with fantasy—leads to nuanced understandings of how talk and text are connected to violence. Moreover, when my students and I think about how organizations communicate, the former position would let us think that organizations do no violence in their communication, and the latter would let us think that organizations can only do violence in their communication. These explanations of the violence–communication relationship provide few resources for organizations, like U.S. universities, that want to prevent and respond to violence. These positions can neither halt a rape epidemic nor fundamentally transform a social structure that visits sexual violence disproportionately on those populations with the least institutional power. To understand how organizations are implicated in violence, we need a different perspective.

Organizations and sexual violence

Despite repeated calls from feminists and critical race scholars to think of violence beyond individual episodes and to focus on the institutional and organizational elements of violence, an organization's role in violence remains difficult to notice. Because people tend to equate violence with immediate bodily injury, we do not learn techniques for noticing what precedes and exceeds those injuries. People attune immediately to physical harm, as good, empathic humans should. But it takes far more analysis, inquiry, and perspective shifting to see something more than solely the decisions an individual rapist makes and the consequences a rapist imposes on the person who survives his violence. Indeed, psychologists and other researchers have shown that it is comforting for humans to assume that people have individual will and that the world is basically a good, just place (K. L. Harris, 2018a). Starting to look beyond the rapist—to the institutional processes and procedures, the public modes of thought, and the social assumptions that surround an instance of rape—can be disquieting and unsettling because it challenges the idea that a few bad apples are to blame for campus sexual assault. In short, locating the organizational elements of sexual violence requires shifting the prevailing sense of the world and coming to grips with difficult realities.

A number of scholars across academic disciplines have noticed that society focuses on bodily harm at the expense of seeing organizational violence. Management scholars Catley and Jones (2002) stated that "decisions are generally made in favour of the representation of violence as an individual physical act . . . This representation has become so widespread that it is often assumed that this is what violence 'really is'" (p. 33). Similarly, philosopher Žižek (2008) observed this trend. He distinguished subjective violence (that experienced by persons) from objective forms of violence (e.g., racist and sexist comments, the effects of capitalism). He argued that scholars and the public tend to focus on the subjective forms of violence and that this focus distracts intellectuals and societies from the objective and systemic forms of violence. In the intellectual pictures that academics and activists alike create, episodes of dyadic violence are so centered and foregrounded that processes of organizational violence are backgrounded at best and, more likely, overlooked altogether.

Nevertheless, some public discussions invite questions about how organizations and sexual violence are related. A recent report showed that U.S. Army personnel committed sexual assault and intimate partner violence at rates that nearly doubled between 2006 and 2011 (U.S. Army, 2012). Further, the rates of sexual violence perpetration were found to be substantially higher in the military than in the civilian population. A different organization, the U.S. Peace Corps, received intense media attention in 2011 following an ABC News report highlighting the organization's poor response to sexual violence that volunteers experienced while serving abroad. This violence became the focus of a U.S. Congressional hearing and prompted the Kate Puzey Peace Corps Volunteer Protection Act. Government agencies are not the only institutions being scrutinized. The Roman Catholic Church has also been the subject of criticism for relocating rather than dismissing priests who are known to sexually assault young church members. In education, too, sexual violence is of public concern. The American Association of University Women released a report claiming that 48% of children and young adults in K–12 education experienced sexual harassment during a single school year (Hill, 2011). In these conversations, the public has grappled with a set of questions: Are organizations or individuals responsible for this violence? How can and should these organizations go about responding to and preventing violence? These implicit questions suggest that the public is interested in thinking about organizational elements of violence.

As that conversation continues—as individuals, groups, and universities continue to think about how to better prevent and respond to sexual violence—they can draw upon ideas from researchers who have already thought about this problem. For instance, organizational studies scholars Hearn and Parkin (2001) developed the concept "organization violation," which includes not only "social enactment" of violence (something akin to my discussion of a moment of rape) but also the "structural presence" of violation, which includes material, symbolic, and historical elements of violence (p. 73). They suggested that violence accumulates through time and that its effects include not only "direct damage" but also "less direct effects, simply through the memory of previous actual or possible violences" (p. xii). Hearn and Parkin, like other scholars who theorize violence, pay attention to more than an individual moment of violence.

Another scholar of organizations, Bessant (1998), proposed the term "opaque violence," and she used it to reference often unnoticed practices including "harassment, surveillance, bullying, interrogation, persecution, victimization, intimidation, and subjugation" that occur in organizations (p. 50). Unlike the term "rape," which is usually associated with bodily contact, "opaque violence" references processes that occur most often without any physical touch. This idea expands the focus of violence beyond the moment of immediately observable harm to human flesh (or at least contact between the flesh of two humans).

In one of very few approaches that focus specifically on discrimination policies—like I do by focusing on Title IX—Spade (2011) used critical race theory and trans politics to identify and explain "administrative violence." Administrative violence occurs when organizations avoid their own culpability by suggesting that violence involves individuals. In other words, Spade illustrates how the very idea that violence is only that which an individual commits can excuse organizations from making important changes. Moreover, that idea keeps in place an organization's ability to support the status quo, particularly around issues of difference including but not limited to cisgenderedness, heteronormativity, whiteness, and hegemonic masculinity.

These existing works from organizational researchers—ones that continue to build a consensus that violence must be understood as not merely the crime an individual commits—provide a starting point for the argument I develop about campus sexual violence. Indeed, they provide part of the groundwork from which I argue that we must learn to think "beyond the rapist."

Beyond the rapist: An overview

In the remainder of the book, I draw together feminist new materialism and an analysis of U.S. campus sexual violence. In Chapter 2, I outline how categorizing something as "violence" depends on assumptions about two concepts: the relationship between physical and symbolic systems (communication), and who or what can act (agency). In Chapter 3, to counter a material–discourse bifurcation, I argue that violence communicates. It does so even when it defies representation. Using diffraction, the primary feminist new materialist method, I show how material–discursive practices continuously organize violence at a university regarded for having some of the most effective sexual violence policies in the United States. In Chapter 4, I analyze how that same university determines who or what can commit violence. I detail the racial and gender dynamics of those decisions, ones that maintain boundaries around the category "human" and therefore influence the organization's relationship to violence. In the final chapter, I offer a summary of the book's arguments. I also apply insights from previous chapters to other contexts, including the violence of organizations that train gymnasts in the United States and violence involving guns. I detail practical suggestions for universities and other organizations that want to intervene in sexual violence more effectively. To close, I highlight the importance and necessity of Title IX processes which provide one mechanism for moving beyond the rapist.

2

An organization's relationship
to violence

*Reading communication and agency
through feminist new materialism*

In his work on violence, Hearn (1998) asserted that people
struggle over how to define violence and that, as they struggle
over definitions, people both reproduce and oppose violence. Building on this assertion, in this chapter, I show how
assumptions about two ideas—communication and agency—are
central to these definitional struggles. Tacit understandings of
communication and agency influence what counts as violence,
how violence comes to be known, where people locate the origins
of violence, and when they think violence terminates. I use feminist new materialism to make these tacit understandings explicit
and also to problematize them. Assumptions about communication and agency also shape how scholars understand the relationship between violence and organization, and feminist new
materialism helps to think through these relationships.

Two approaches to communication and agency—ones I in-
troduce via caricature—often surface in public and scholarly
debates about violence. On the one hand, if I assume that communication merely represents the world, I separate the symbolic from the physical. Communication is reduced to a mirror,

one that can reflect but not impact the world. Because words do not act, they are somewhat impotent: They can describe violence but never enact it. In this view, organizations only speak about violence. They either describe sexual assault accurately or they do not. On the other hand, if I assume that communication completely constitutes the world, then I miss reality. From this approach, much like pop culture's *The Secret*, I can talk things into being regardless of external circumstances. When I speak, I am omnipotent. In this view, a person needs only to say "no" to stop a rapist's attack and organizations need only to declare they will not tolerate sexual assault in order to end campus rape.

To rethink the violence–organization relationship—and to resist the institutionalization of sexual violence—scholars and activists need a view of communication and agency different from either of these preceding caricatures. As the chapter proceeds, I develop this different view by reading feminist new materialism and communication studies through one another. I pursue a feminist new materialist understanding of communication that is neither wholly correspondent—as in the first caricatured view—nor wholly constitutive—as in the second. This understanding of communication is nascent but not yet realized in feminist new materialist theorizing. I also push communication scholarship toward a feminist new materialist approach to agency. This understanding of agency resists anthropocentrism, thinks beyond the liberal subject, and pays careful attention to power and difference. By drawing communication and agency to the fore, I develop a feminist new materialist understanding of the violence–organization relationship, one in which rape—like other kinds of violence—is an intertwined material–discursive phenomenon. Moreover, from this view, rape is no longer solely an individual's action, but the accumulation of organizational actions. I begin by examining public arguments in which organizations are actors and communication is both symbolic and material.

The idea that nonhuman entities (or organizations) can act—and even speak—is not far from mainstream discourse. Indeed, these notions circulate extensively in public conversations about the 2010 U.S. Supreme Court decision, *Citizens United v. Federal Election Commission*. The case granted First Amendment rights to corporations for purposes of political campaign spending, and the decision became famously controversial for eliding corporations and persons. At the time, one political cartoon showed James Madison's hand penning "We the people," then crossing out "people" and replacing it with "corporations." As the drawing suggests, the court's ruling seemed to assign certain human capabilities to organizations. Granting corporations some of the same rights as individual human beings is not unusual, and courts in the United States have done so for more than 100 years. The trouble around this case, however, stemmed from its near conflation of money, speech, and personhood.

The court judged that limits on corporate spending for political messages, including television ads, would effectively limit speech. Though common sense says communication is merely symbolic, common sense also suggests that money has material impacts. It can accumulate disproportionately and proffer the benefits of wealth to particular entities, persons and organizations alike. Many communication scholars have criticized the decision's deleterious effects on democracy (e.g., Thimsen, 2015). I would add that the uproar over the case was so loud because members of the public readily recognize that speech—including paid messaging—is *not* merely symbolic. When a particular organization is able to pay for myriad advertisements, the proliferation of those television or radio spots is material in and of itself. The ads' amplification of particular positions then influences voting and policy decisions, and, in turn, those votes and policies impact bodies and access to resources. I review all this to say that the idea that nonhumans can act—and moreover that communication involves more than symbols—is not far from general consciousness.

Space for understanding organizations as actors and for understanding communication as both material and discursive is available in public discourse, but applying these ideas to violence is not so easy. Though people sometimes accept that organizations are actors, it is more difficult to assert that organizations are violent actors. The *Citizens United* decision solidifies organizations as discursive actors—speakers—but sets no limits on an organization's "spoken" actions. This lack of limitation suggests an underlying disconnect between discourse and materiality: If speech could do material harm, *Citizens United* might have put some boundaries around how much and how often an organization's money can "speak." This presumed separation between discourse—spoken action—and material harm also plays out in popular understandings of violence. The public generally still thinks of violence as an event that one human enacts, and the violence consists of physical, material harm to another individual person. For instance, few people doubt that when members of the Catholic Church's clergy sexually assaulted boys, those clergy members committed violence. Members of the public seem less clear, though, about whether the church itself committed violence either before or after those discrete incidents of assault.

In sum, people most readily notice violence and label it as such when one human causes physical harm or destruction to another. Catley and Jones (2002) made this argument: "Violence takes many forms, but when it appears in a 'sovereign' act of individual physical violence it is obvious, and recognised as being violent. When violence is symbolic or structural it tends to disappear from view" (p. 34). In this rendering, two problems obscure violence. First, violence is overwhelmingly understood as physical.

Second, violence is understood as individual. Feminist new materialism provides an avenue for thinking about, challenging, and reframing these assumptions. As I argue below, these problems are about communication (the physical–symbolic relationship) and agency (who or what can act and whether action resides in individuals). To begin reading feminist new materialism and communication scholarship through one another, I next outline the distinctive features of feminist new materialism.

Feminist new materialism's distinctive features

In the last chapter, I outlined feminist new materialism's unusual orientation to time. Its peculiar temporality shapes the stories feminists tell about it, ones that often emphasize discontinuities and indeterminacies. Stephens (2014), for instance, said that "feminist new materialism is like fluidity itself: it remains a constitutively ambiguous category, less a coherent disciplinary field than a collection of often contradictory or disparate works" (pp. 186–187). Even as it challenges hard boundaries around disciplines and traditions, feminist new materialism's postures are unique. Dolphijn and van der Tuin (2012) described it as "a distinctive trend" and also a "tool for opening up theory formation" (p. 100). Detailing its defining characteristics and lineages is, of course, a deeply political task. Some readers will find hints of Marx, Austin, Deleuze, Derrida, Guattari, Foucault, DeLanda, Leibniz, and Spinoza, but I have cited none of these men in this section. Instead, I have amplified and authorized this story of feminist new materialism via the likes of Butler, Barad, van der Tuin, Wiegman, Minh-ha, Grosz, Crenshaw, and Matsuda, among others. As I continue in this section, I trace feminist new materialism's relationships with these feminist thinkers in order to orient and historicize feminist new materialism, but the story is not and cannot be comprehensive. Others have documented the archives and genealogies of feminist new materialism, and readers seeking a more detailed overview should consult that work (e.g., Coole & Frost, 2010; Hird, 2004; Jagger, 2015). In brief, the distinctive features of feminist new materialism include (a) developing a tradition that is neither social constructivist nor realist, (b) conceptualizing the material as agentic and independent of human action, (c) understanding discourse as nonhuman and material, and (d) emphasizing posthumanism.

(a) Social constructivism versus realism: Reworking the "versus"

The origin stories about feminist theories often begin from a split between sex—a biological identity—and gender—a learned identity. To discard the idea that women were naturally and inevitably imbued with certain, narrow characteristics—obsequiousness, sentimentality, and a propensity for domestic labor—many feminists argued that gender was developed socially. They emphasized that femininity was not the result of hormones, diminutive upper bodies, or a uterus. As many have noted, this sex/gender separation was politically generative, but it also required feminism to de-emphasize sex—or nature—and focus on gender—or culture (Fraser, 2002). This often-told account about feminism's indebtedness to social construction and its overlap with a linguistic turn is not the whole story. Even while relying on construction, feminists have always been attentive to materiality and the empirical world. They have developed sophisticated theories of bodies (e.g., Grosz, 1994), accounted for the economic conditions that underwrite gendered and raced inequalities (e.g., McCall, 2001), and demonstrated the realness of oppression. These twin interests—making gender pliable while also solidifying evidence of patriarchy—have led many to tell a story about feminism's paradoxes (Scott, 1997), the inevitable contradictions that arise when a field "traverses" both "(biological) essentialism and social construction" (Dolphijn & van der Tuin, 2012, p. 138). Elsewhere, I argued that these seeming inconsistencies are better understood as dilemmas, ones at the core of a nascent feminist new materialism (K. L. Harris, 2016a). As a whole, the emerging tradition identifies and then alters "the commonalities of realism and social constructivism" (Dolphijn & van der Tuin, 2012, p. 98). By reworking seeming oppositions between dominant approaches to knowledge and truth, feminist new materialism calls forth a tradition that is neither wholly constructivist nor wholly realist.

(b) The material is articulate and agentic, independent of humans

Some scholars have argued that feminist new materialism seems "new" only if it erases the ever-present focus on materiality in feminist scholarship. Indeed, some accounts of feminist new materialism seem to argue that feminism has under-theorized the material (e.g., Alaimo & Hekman, 2008). Clare (2016) rightly noted that this origin story requires amnesia about intersectionality, feminist phenomenology, and Marxist feminisms. Furthermore, it requires overlooking key contributions from numerous feminists such as Delphy (1977), Hartsock (1983), and Crenshaw (1989). Yet in keeping with the meaning of "new" I outlined in the last chapter, feminist new materialism is not about correcting feminism's past omissions. Instead, feminist new materialism acknowledges, as Hinton and van der Tuin (2014) said, that "the political in its feminist incarnations has always been shot through with material dynamics" (p. 2). Feminist new materialism has not suddenly brought feminist attention to the material. For decades, feminists have paid careful attention to the material dynamics of gender, power, and oppression.

Feminist new materialism builds on this longstanding tradition and nudges it toward something different by refusing to separate the material from the discursive. Barad (2003) confronted one common misreading of the emerging new materialist tradition: "The point [of feminist new materialism] is not merely that there are important material factors in addition to discursive ones" (p. 823). This idea is already well established in feminist thinking. Instead, feminist new materialism seeks to undermine further the separations between the natural (material) and the social (discursive). As Barad (2003) went on to say, the focus is on how to theorize "the conjoined material–discursive nature of constraints, conditions, and practices" (p. 823). Similarly, Grosz (2017) argued that the material is ideal, and the ideal is material. Feminist new materialism continues a feminist tradition of theorizing the material and, simultaneously, it shifts what the material means and how it comes to matter.

Feminists have long disrupted Cartesian dualism's separation between meaning and matter, and feminist new materialism amplifies that project. Frost (2011) noted that feminists drawing on Marxism made important interventions in a Cartesian worldview. They showed how "the products of labor become constitutive elements of the economic and political structures that direct, constrain, and compel individuals' behavior" (p. 73). In this approach to gender, matter and material is somewhat agentic: It accumulates human activities and then, in turn, shapes individuals' lives. Yet in Marxist feminisms, and historical materialism more broadly, the agency of matter remains a product of human activity. By contrast, feminist new materialism moves away from anthropocentrism, and the goal is to develop theory in which matter's agency is not dependent on humans.

Feminist new materialism's understanding of materiality is also indebted to Butler's (1993) influential arguments that deny bodies' independence from discourse. Though Butler challenged the discourse–materiality divide, many feminist new materialists have argued that body/mind, nature/culture, and matter/discourse dualisms can and should still be more fully undone. Although appreciative of *Bodies that Matter*, N. Davis (2009) said that Butler's theories of discourse are nevertheless primarily cultural and that "the physical . . . remains outside the social" (p. 78). Summarizing a stronger critique, van der Tuin and Dolphijn (2010) referenced "a feminist polemic against the failed materialism in the work of Judith Butler" (p. 154). To more fully integrate the physical and the social, feminist new materialists have extended and critiqued Butler's work by decentering human action. Barad (2003), for example, borrowed aspects of Butler's performativity and then worked it through posthumanism in order to develop something distinct, yet in the spirit of transposition (see Chapter 1), related. This push toward material agency, independent of humans, is one component of feminist new materialism's distinctiveness.

(c) Discursive practices are material and nonhuman: Theorizing intra-actions

To more fully challenge the discourse–material split, Barad (2003) argued that discourse–materiality constantly intra-acts and explained,

> Materiality is discursive (i.e., material phenomena are inseparable from the apparatuses of bodily production: matter emerges out of and includes as part of its being the ongoing reconfiguring of boundaries), just as discursive practices are always already material (i.e., they are ongoing material (re)

configurings of the world). Discursive practices and material
phenomena do not stand in a relationship of externality to
one another; rather, the material and the discursive are mutually implicated in the dynamics of intra-activity. (p. 822)

In this rendering, discourse–materiality enfolds itself, and it is
no longer sufficient for scholars to speak of discourse *and* materiality because the two cannot be meaningfully separated. Feminist
new materialists do not advocate simply identifying the material
impacts of discourse or the discursive impacts of the material, as
these renderings preserve a prior split between the two. Instead,
they generate theory, method, and modes of being in which discourse materializes and matter engages meaning.

This intra-active approach further distinguishes feminist
new materialism from Butler's (1993; 1997) important work.
Whereas Butler relied extensively on Austin's speech acts, Barad
(2003) said directly, "Discursive practices are not speech acts"
(p. 821). Instead, they are the "material conditions for making
meaning" (Barad, 2007, p. 335). Barad makes this claim because discourse cannot be separated from the material world.
Moreover, many scholars note that Butler's work located agency
in culture (e.g., Cheah, 1996; N. Davis, 2009). By contrast, in
feminist new materialism, particularly Barad's iteration of it, the
world becomes—and becomes something different—through
continuous and ongoing material–discursive intra-actions that
are not dependent on human action.

When matter is "not a thing, but a doing" and discourse is
a "boundary-making practice," discourse–materiality loses
some inertia and solidity (Barad, 2003, p. 822). In scholarship
that draws upon these principles, the "object" of study shifts.
Researchers address the intra-active processes through which
phenomena continuously come into being. Scholars do not
suddenly start focusing on so-called material "things" such as

bananas or phones or limestone. Instead, the discursive–material practices that enact boundaries around the supposedly separate material or discourse come to the fore of method, analysis, and writing. As Barad (2003) noted, when a boundary emerges, it "always entails constitutive exclusions and therefore requisite questions of accountability" (p. 803). As feminist new materialism sets the boundaries around discourse and materiality in motion, it foregrounds questions about who or what is left out when phenomena materialize.

(d) Nonhumans act: Decentering the humanist subject

Per feminist new materialism, humans are not in charge of material–discursive intra-actions, and they do not independently drive the world's becoming. As Frost (2011) noted, "New materialists push feminists to decenter human intentionality and design in the conceptualization of the relationship between nature and culture" (p. 77). Feminist new materialism's resulting focus on post-, non-, and extra-humans is one of its primary distinctions from its other materialist feminist forebears. Feminist new materialism has emerged through conversation with physics, technology studies, environmental studies, and other sciences where sharp boundaries around entities are increasingly problematized. Like poststructuralist feminisms, feminist new materialists emphasize the ongoing becoming of what only appears to be a stable, coherent subject. But whereas the unstable subject remains a product of human activity in many iterations of poststructuralist thought—that is, an effect of human discourse—feminist new materialism takes a slightly different approach. It questions the line between "human" and "nonhuman" altogether. As Barad (2003) said, "the very practices by which the differential boundaries of the 'human' and the

'nonhuman' are drawn are always already implicated in particular materializations" (p. 824). "Human" is in a process of con-
tinual becoming, constituted via constant material–discursive
intra-actions.

These distinctive features of feminist new materialism—
developing a third way between constructivism and realism,
locating materiality's agentic and discursive capacities, and
fostering politically generative posthuman theory—resonate
with existing scholarship in communication studies and organizational communication. To draw out these resonances, I read my
discipline's extensive theorizing of two terms—communication
and agency—through feminist new materialism.

Communication as material–discursive intra-action: Resonances between communication studies and feminist new materialism

I use the word "communication" to signal an unsettled, open
question: How are the symbolic and physical worlds related?
The discipline of communication studies offers ambiguous and
seemingly contradictory answers to this question, answers that
resonate with feminist new materialist theory. In some of the
field's most influential texts, scholars detail seemingly diver-
gent approaches. For some writers, communication occurs when
people use symbols to describe the physical world. For others,
people use symbols to impact, evoke, or even make the physical
world. Carey (2009) detailed the former position at length:

> Both our common sense and scientific realism attest to the
> fact that there is, first, a real world of objects, events, and
> processes that we observe. Second, there is language or

symbols that name these events in the real world and create more or less adequate descriptions of them. There is reality and then, after the fact, our accounts of it. We insist there is a distinction between reality and fantasy; we insist that our terms stand in relation to this world as shadow and substance. While language often distorts, obfuscates, and confuses our perception of this external world, we rarely dispute this matter-of-fact realism. We peel away semantic layers of terms and meanings to uncover this more substantial domain of existence. (p. 25)

In this passage, Carey offers a more nuanced description of the caricature I introduced earlier in this chapter, one in which communication symbolizes the world while standing apart from it. He is one of many scholars who has described a similar approach to communication that members of my discipline variously refer to as transmissive, representative, or correspondent.

Even as he outlines this position, Carey argues vociferously against it and, indeed, playfully reverses it. He quips, with the help of St. John and Burke, that the word was first, that "things are the signs of words" (p. 25). In this alternative perspective, the world follows the word. These claims align with the second caricature I offered at the opening of the chapter in which communication does everything.

As I hinted earlier, the academic field of communication studies dances somewhere in between these two caricatures. These moves are evident in Carey's work when he argues neither that words entirely make the world nor that symbols are everything. He is careful to note that "communication" always operates in dual senses: as something that represents the world and also as something that impacts what happens in that world. Carey uses a house blueprint to illustrate his position: When language provides a representation *of* reality, "If someone asks for a description of a particular house, one can simply point to a blue-print and say, 'That's the house'" (p. 29). When language provides a representation *for* reality, "Under [the blueprint's] guidance and control a reality, a house, is produced that expresses the rela-tions contained in reduced and simplified form in the blueprint" (p. 29). The blueprint symbolizes something in the world, and it also provides directions for how to make the world.

Like many other communication scholars, Carey works against the idea that symbolic and physical worlds can be use-fully understood as entirely distinct. Many people in the field of communication refuse an easy binary between subject and object, culture and nature, body and mind, material and dis-course. Indeed, Craig (1999) argued that one central purpose of the discipline is to evoke doubt about a representationalist approach to communication, one in which words merely trans-port information about the world from place to place. The field resists this common-sense model of communication because it neatly separates words from the facts of reality. It makes com-munication both straightforward and insignificant, and words and world remain distinct. This impulse—to grant communi-cation some creative and active capacity, to challenge the con-ceptual division between discourse and materiality while not abandoning reality—patterns communication theorizing. It should also sound quite similar to the new materialist principles I outlined earlier in this chapter. Barad (2003) is not a commu-nication scholar, but she issued a similar critique of "the repre-sentationalist belief in the power of words to mirror preexisting phenomena" (p. 802). The central problem for the field of com-munication is intricately related to feminist new materialists' more explicitly political rendering of an emerging tradition that is neither strictly constructivist nor realist. Given that the field of communication studies and feminist new materialist theory grapple with similar problematics, what better place to continue developing feminist new materialism than in communication studies?

Perhaps nowhere is the field of communication's consistent attention to the relationship between the physical and material worlds more persistent and purposeful than in feminist communication theory. Though Craig (1999) averred that the field of communication's "central intellectual role" and "cultural mission" is to challenge representationalism (p. 125), for feminists the goal is different. Intersectional theorists and scholars, in particular, simultaneously retain and reject representationalist approaches to communication. As McCall (2005) described, scholars who adopt intersectional methods keep the negative impacts of racism–sexism in view and also cast doubt upon the inevitability of the categories that produce those differences. They do so by using symbols to point at the real world while also troubling the correspondence between those symbols and the world. On the whole, feminist communication scholars prioritize the seeming contradictions—better understood as dilemmas—that arise from both utilizing and problematizing representationalism (K. L. Harris, 2016a; 2016b). The interplay of these two modes—representationalist and constitutive—calls forth a different politics, one from which feminist new materialism emerges in communication studies.

Feminists' double goals for communication—to describe and transform the world—operate within a field that has for decades relied heavily, if not exclusively, on social construction. And yet feminists' relationship to social construction is uneasy. To adopt an extreme social constructivist stance would mean allowing facts to be always pliable fictions. But to abandon the pliability that comes with social construction would mean letting go of the potential for discourse to fundamentally change the world we live in. Hekman (2009), a political scientist, explained feminism's peculiar relationship to social construction well:

> First, feminists want to be able to talk about the reality of women's bodies and their lived experiences in a patriarchal world. Extreme linguistic determinism precludes such discussions. Second, feminists want to assert the truth of their statements regarding women's status in that world. Embracing social constructionism and the relativism that it entails makes it impossible to make such truth claims. (p. 107)

As Hekman noted, some versions of social construction could undermine feminism's political goals. But social construction also provides the means by which feminists subvert troubling arguments that gender is natural and, therefore, fixed. Alaimo (2011) argued that if feminists do not challenge matter's presumed insulation from the symbolic world, then "female bodies continue to be cast as the dumb matter that male intellect seeks to escape. Moreover, the intersecting categories of race and class have also been constituted by their pernicious associations with brute matter" (p. 281). Feminist communication scholars cannot walk away from social construction altogether. To do so would mean giving up some of the tenets that make the field important. If communication does not in some way *make* reality, scholars would have few reasons to study it at all.

The approaches to communication I have outlined—and especially feminist approaches to communication—unravel a neat separation between subject and object, discourse and material. Instead, they provide a framework that centers the complex and ongoing intertwining of word and world. They already reverberate with feminist new materialism, and those reverberations are important for understanding violence and organizations. Without this approach that fuses communication studies and feminist new materialist principles, an organization's connection to violence is merely managerial: When symbols and physical events are distinct, the organization is merely a thing that counts assaults and makes decisions about how to respond after violence has happened. It is hard—if not impossible—to think about how the organization may *enact* violence. To address this aspect of the organization's relationship to violence with more complexity, the organization must be not only a communicator, but also an actor. To understand it as such, scholars need nontraditional approaches to agency.

Agency beyond the human: Resonances between organizational communication and feminist new materialism

I use the term "agency" to reference the process via which the world comes into being through continuous material–discursive intra-actions. In an interview with Dolphijn and van der Tuin (2012), Barad said that agency is "about the possibilities and accountability entailed in reconfiguring material–discursive apparatuses of bodily production, including the boundary articulations and exclusions that are marked by those practices" (p. 54). In Barad's articulation of agency, she pays close attention to the ways in which phenomena emerge, how boundaries coalesce around phenomena, and what or who is set aside in that process.

This understanding of agency is different from many dominant understandings of the term. Unlike the feminist new materialist iteration of the term, "agency" usually references the intentional, rational, conscious decision of a human. K. K. Campbell (2005) noted that this prevailing understanding of agency relies on "a concept of the individual that did not emerge fully in the West until late in the sixteenth or early in the seventeenth century" (p. 2). In keeping with that period of history, this traditional understanding of agency retains the idea that humans are both autonomous and free-willed. Furthermore, a split between the physical and discursive worlds accompanies this understanding. After thinking carefully about the best course of action, a person then influences the world in order to create a desired outcome. The former process is presumed to be discursive or symbolic, the latter material or physical. This longstanding approach to agency does not hold under feminist new materialism.

Scholars who resist a feminist new materialist approach to agency claim that it vitiates politics. Characterizing this position, Bennett (2005) said, "the fear is that to distribute agency more widely would be to jeopardize attempts to hold individuals responsible for their actions or to hold officials accountable to the public" (p. 452). Under less individualized understandings of agency, like those of feminist new materialism, societies cannot hold only one person responsible for particular actions, and social change cannot depend solely on humans' moral choices (Caldwell, 2007; Cooper, 2011).

In the context of rape on campuses, these concerns about a feminist new materialist approach to agency are serious. The U.S. judicial system already rarely holds perpetrators accountable for rape. Few cases are reported, fewer still go to trial, and even fewer result in convictions. Given this context, I understand why some scholars are uneasy with a version of agency that seems to make it even more difficult to punish individuals for wrongdoing. To complicate the matter further, our current understanding of agency also makes it hard to see systems beyond individuals. When a person appears to be held accountable for rape, sometimes what we are really seeing is legally sanctioned injustice fueled by racist accusations and systemic oppression. For example, in 1984, an all-white jury wrongfully convicted Darryl Hunt, a black man, of raping and murdering a white woman. He served 19 years in prison before being exonerated. Under prevailing understandings of agency, we are neither punishing rapists nor stopping campus sexual violence, and we are also not doing a good job of thinking through the systemic dynamics of sexual violence, including the relationships between sexual violence and racism.

Despite these risks, conceptualizing agency beyond individual humans can enhance feminist projects. Importantly, a feminist new materialist account of agency refuses to minimize the complexity of sexual violence, and it requires careful consideration of the parts of the world that people commonly exclude from their understanding of this problem. It interrupts a system that first sorts the good from the bad and uses the resulting sharp line between the two to govern responses to rape. Rather than shutting off the possibility of political action, some feminist new materialists—including me—believe this reworking of agency expands, rather than undermines, avenues for transforming the world. Reflecting this line of thought, Bennett (2005) noted:

> It is ultimately a matter of political judgment what is more needed today: Should we acknowledge the distributive quality of agency in order to address the power of human–nonhuman assemblages and to resist a politics of blame? Or should we persist with a strategic understatement of material agency in the hope of enhancing the accountability of specific humans? (p. 464)

On the whole, feminist new materialists respond to this query by rejecting the strategic understatement of material agency. In subsequent chapters, I advocate for a more distributed understanding of agency because it points to the material–discursive processes via which boundaries around sexual violence come into being. I also issue cautions about dampening the agency of discourse.

A feminist new materialist understanding of agency resonates with organizational communication scholarship in which robust conversations about textual and nonhuman agencies have developed. For example, Brummans (2007) described how the euthanasia order that his family members signed exerted influence on his father's death:

> As a nonhuman agent among human agents, the text projected the end of my dad's life from the past, creating a field of action that was demarcated by whom we had thought to be and were—a space that felt surreal, but was real. Thus, the text helped to create a kind of bubble, defining our hemispheres by giving us the freedom to commit an act, the legality of which is questioned in most countries, but also making us prisoners of our own word. Were we "disobedient" when we acted out of line with the text, for example, by not deciding to proceed with the euthanasia when my dad was no longer capable of going to the toilet by himself or when he became delusional—a line we once drew? (p. 723)

In this passage, Brummans traces the decision-making processes of human agents who solidify their agreements in a text. Later, that text exerts influence on those humans. Brummans makes clear that the text is not a sole agent: It does not simply determine that his father should receive a fatal injection at the first moment that fits the conditions to which the human agents had agreed. Instead, the text becomes merely one actor among humans and nonhumans alike, and both shape how and when his father died. The euthanasia agreement, which speaks as a character in the article, says, "I helped kill a man spoken for" (p. 721). The text itself does not kill a human: The family doctor delivers the lethal dose of medicine. But the text is nonetheless involved in that human's death. The phrase "man spoken for" blurs the lines between who speaks, when, on behalf of whom. Actions and speakers become muddled and are no longer discrete, no longer owned by any individual, no longer located in one moment in time.

Documents' influence on the continuous processes that make an organization is often called "textual agency" (Cooren, 2004). Much like the way the euthanasia agreement operated in Brummans' piece, the texts that Cooren discussed continue to leave traces long after they are created: "Signs, memos, and contracts display a form of agency by doing things that humans alone could not do . . . [they] participate in the channeling of behaviors, constitute and stabilize organizational pathways, and broadcast information/orders" (p. 388). Without these texts, organizations would not be as effective. Organizational texts exert force on humans, even as humans create and use these texts. For instance, employment contracts create a reference point that shapes but does not dictate the ongoing decisions of both employee and employer about pay, duties, expectations, and termination. By drawing textual and human agency together, Cooren argued that the provenance of action is plural: "Humans are acted upon as well as acting through the textual and physical objects they produce. They enter into a chain of actions that extend beyond their original contributions" (p. 388). In other words, human agency alone does not provide an adequate framework for understanding the actions of organizations. On this point, feminist new materialists and these organizational communication scholars are in agreement.

Though similar in their assertion that agency is both human and nonhuman, Brummans' and Cooren's discussions depart from feminist new materialist accounts of agency in one key way: Their primary goal is not to delineate how difference and inequity are implicated in texts' agencies, and their arguments can appear to be politically neutral. Elsewhere in organizational communication, Broadfoot and Munshi (2015) provided an important reminder to readers that, despite appearing neutral, concepts cannot escape power dynamics. They asserted that the version of agency one adopts is both shaped by and shapes the world. Indeed, recognizing the importance and impact of scholarly concepts, organizational scholars who focus on corporate social responsibility suggested that expanded understandings of agency—ones I believe to be similar to the ones feminist new materialism can offer—are necessary for addressing social problems (e.g., Gerencser, 2005; May, Cheney, & Roper, 2007). Given these provocations and my own feminist commitments, I hope for more explicit engagement with politics and difference in organizational scholarship on nonhuman agency. Nonetheless, existing work such as that of Brummans and Cooren provides an important link between existing organizational scholarship and the nascent feminist new materialist perspectives I seek to invite more fully into the field of communication. Both approaches challenge the anthropocentrism of dominant understandings of agency and begin to tell a more complicated story about action.

A feminist new materialist understanding of agency poses fundamental challenges to readily available understandings of violence. First, this view of agency disarticulates violence from intention and instead posits violence as an outcome of complex material–discursive processes that extend beyond an individual person. Uncoupled from discrete human entities, this iteration of agency opens possibilities for rethinking the violence–organization relationship. Similar to scholarship that adopts social constructivist positions, especially Butler's extension of Austin's speech acts, a feminist new materialist understanding of agency asserts that words and language act on and influence the material world. But a feminist new materialist understanding of agency departs from the well-known work on speech acts in an important way. Because feminist new materialism rejects a clear division between human and nonhuman, it complicates who or what can speak. Speech has often been a precursor for being human and for having agency, and in Chapters 3 and 4 I delve more fully into the troubling elisions of these terms.

How are violence and organization related?

The approaches to communication and agency that I have detailed—ones that fuse feminist new materialism and theorizing from my disciplinary home—are particularly consequential for conceptualizing the relationship between violence and organizations. If I adopt the dominant or common-sense understandings of communication and agency—that communication is only symbolic, that agency is the action of an individual human—I can render the relationship between violence and organization only in limited ways. But if I adopt some of the perspectives I have outlined, that relationship looks more intricate. In existing research, scholars suggest either that violence occurs *in* an organization or that violence is one component *of* organizations. Each perspective carries implicit assumptions about how the material and discursive worlds are connected and who or what can act, and each provides some useful starting points for how I theorize the relationship between sexual violence and U.S. universities in subsequent chapters.

Violence in organization

At face value, if one assumes that violence occurs in an organization, the organization has a negligible or nonexistent role in that violence. The organization is merely the site at which violence occurs. Chamberlain, Crowley, Tope, and Hodson's (2008) statement about sexual harassment—one form of sexual violence—reflected this approach: "individuals act out sexual harassment, [and] they do so *within the context of organizations*" (p. 263, emphasis added). In other words, the organization is incidental, and human agents commit violence. Summarizing this perspective in existing research, Catley (2005) said, "violence is cast as a problem *for* organisations rather than a problem *of* organisation" (p. 8). When an organization is the container for humans' violent acts, organizations cannot be agents of violence.

Yet even when scholars define violence as an individual human action—and seem to write off the possibility that organizations commit violence—they still identify a role that organizations play: The organization can influence whether individuals enact violence. For example, Chamberlain et al. (2008) argued that "organizational context governs whether and how sexual harassment actually transpires in a given workplace" (p. 265). Arguments like these—that organizational characteristics can influence whether violence occurs—have led some scholars to identify conditions under which violence is likely in an organization. Salin (2003), for example, suggested that organizations with marked power differences tend to have high levels of harassment and aggression. Extreme power differences can occur when majority identity groups have more resources and when management styles are authoritarian. If organizational members are also unhappy and frustrated, or if competition among organizational members is prevalent, these behaviors are even more likely. Furthermore, organizations experiencing crisis or significant change often find amplified levels of harassment. Some existing research, like Salin's, offers detailed accounts of organizational factors—both contextual and circumstantial—that increase the likelihood of violence.

Many other scholars have also identified organizational structures and power dynamics that make harassment likely. Clair (1993a; 1993b) showed that bureaucratic processes such as reporting allow organizations to maintain and frame harassment as a private experience. Similarly, Conrad and Taylor (1994) suggested that isolation of organizational members who experience violence contributes to harassment's prevalence. The informal climates of many organizations deter those on the receiving end of aggressive behavior from speaking about it, and many organizations shroud investigations into these behaviors in secrecy, often because they are considered personnel matters. These patterns of speech and silence are shaped, as Lutgen-Sandvik and Tracy (2011) argued in their study of workplace bullying, by three levels of communication: micro-discourses, or interactions between individuals; meso-discourses, or "organizational climate, culture, policies, and procedures" (p. 7); and macro-discourses, or society-wide systems of meaning that condone bullying. Among these scholars who imply that violence is something a human does, organizational characteristics make those humans more or less likely to commit violent acts. Though organizations do not commit violence, they can influence it.

Together, these studies emphasize the organizational characteristics that influence the likelihood of violence in organizations. These studies do not go so far as to suggest that organizational processes *are* violence. As such, they retain some of the popular assumptions that I have outlined, namely that violence is physical and the product of individual human action. Nevertheless, these studies provide an important entry point for suggesting that organizations are involved in violence, not simply incidental to it.

Violence of organization

From a different perspective, some scholars assume that organizations are violent, but they do not necessarily assume that organizations enact violence. This group of thinkers presumes that violence is an intrinsic component of all social order. They assert that life is characterized by chaos, and they argue that any process of organization necessarily involves violence (e.g., Bergin & Westwood, 2003; Westwood, 2003). These scholars do not identify elements of organizations that make violence likely because they assert that all organizations are inherently violent. The underlying assumption of this strand of scholarship is rarely explicitly stated: Violence is organizing/ordering and organizing/ordering is violent.

In this strand of research, "violence" does not indicate physical injury to humans. Instead, violence—or order—opposes natural, social chaos. Anytime society moves away from its original unstructured form, violence occurs. The moral overtone of this definition of violence is quite different from that of mainstream definitions: Violence is infused with transformative potential. As Bergin and Westwood (2003) stated, violence is "productive and creative, providing the means by which the new becomes a possibility and the prisons of convention and orthodoxy [are] challenged" (p. 217). Additionally, Pelzer (2003) attested that violence necessitates organizations because organizations can contain and limit violence.

I appreciate that these scholars challenge the dominant, unexamined, often implicit assumption that violence is always bad and wrong. But their definition of violence is not one I adopt because it does not focus on how difference and inequity are connected to violence. Without a nuanced analysis of power, these perspectives cannot advance the kinds of judgments I find necessary in a world patterned by racial, gendered, and sexualized differences. Nevertheless, some elements of this perspective are useful because they move violence out of the moment of bodily injury.

Though a minority of scholars assumes that all organization is violent, one implication of their perspective has been quite influential. Specifically, if violence does not occur at a single moment in time and is not a localized event, organizational processes can then be considered part of the enactment of violence. For example, Hearn and Parkin (2001) adopted some of these assumptions to develop the idea of *organization violation*. Organization violations include those "structures, actions, events and experiences that violate or cause violation. Violence then goes beyond physical violence . . . to include intimidation, surveillance, persecution, subjugation, oppression, discrimination, misrepresentation and exclusion" (Hearn, 2003, p. 254). This focus on organizational processes, including many of the items on this list, is amenable to a feminist new materialist framework. Surveillance, for instance, is not a function of an individual human. Similarly challenging the notion that violence is discrete, Dougherty and Smythe (2004) showed how sexual harassment is diffused throughout an organization's culture. Other communication scholars noted that contradictions in an organization's culture, its policies, and its responses to harassment often function to maintain a hostile climate (Dougherty & Goldstein Hode, 2016; Violanti, 1996). Work such as this suggests that violence is woven through organizational processes and dynamics, not that it simply occurs in an organization.

The violence *of* organization perspective usefully complicates definitions of violence. "Violence" does not signal only an individual's attempts to injure another human. It becomes less discrete and less immediate. From this perspective, it is possible for the organization to be a violent actor and to participate in ongoing physical–symbolic processes connected to violence.

Conclusion

In sum, debates over the definition of violence matter. To think beyond the rapist, it is useful to notice the concepts implicated— but rarely identified—in those struggles: communication and agency. These terms are interrelated, and both concepts have consequences for not only what counts as violence, but also what organizations can do about it. These two terms are the focal points for Chapter 3 and Chapter 4, respectively. In the next chapter on communication, I use diffraction—the primary method of feminist new materialism—to analyze and critique struggles over the prevalence of rape on U.S. campuses. In so doing, I argue that violence communicates in ways that defy representation. I focus not on the messages of a rapist, a victim, or an organization but instead on the complex, material–discursive intra-actions through which organizational processes of sexual violence become intelligible.

3

Violence communicates differently

Diffraction and the organization of rape

In her foundational text on trauma studies, Herman (1997) summarized her project: "I have tried to find a language that . . . allows all of us to come a little closer to facing the unspeakable" (p. 4). She suggested that assault, abuse, and torture cannot be described. Throughout her book, Herman meditated on the "wordlessness of trauma" (p. 158), and this notion that violence cannot speak permeates many areas of scholarship. Ricoeur (1998), for example, said that violence opposes language: "A violence that speaks is already a violence trying to be right: it is a violence that places itself in the orbit of reason and that already is beginning to negate itself as violence" (p. 33). By this line of thought, violence defies speech, words, and language.

The same assumptions operate in feminist antiviolence work. Raine (1998) wrote a widely read book about her experiences following sexual assault, and the title, *After Silence*, evokes this idea. Likewise, in her book *Organizing Silence*, Clair (1998) argued that sexual harassment silences marginalized members of organizations. Both titles imply that the unsaid is a product of sexual violence, and silence can support systems of assault. It follows that paying attention to silences and talking about assaults is a form of resistance. Similarly, people who experience rape often say they become a survivor, no longer a victim, when they speak out.

Saying something about assault is akin to triumph over base, immoral acts. Indeed, in her book on the violence surrounding the 1947 Partition of India, Das (2007) noted, "There is even something heroic in the image of empowering women to speak" (p. 57). Some feminists suggest that, through speech, society can aspire toward ever more truthful accounts of the world. Talk can overcome violence: So the story goes.

Rendered thusly, violence stands on one side of a gulf that separates it from speech, language, talk, and often "discourse." This commonplace appears so often in discussions of violence that it goes almost without notice. Speech becomes the antithesis of assault, and it assumes an emancipatory patina. When scholars and activists claim that rape creates silence, that trauma is wordless, that language opposes violence, their claims are not about communication in the sense that I outlined in the last chapter. Instead, they reference one side of a persistent bifurcation. When sexual violence is conceptualized in this way, organizations' first responses to rape usually involve figuring out how often sexual violence happens and then using those counts to guide other action. As the chapter progresses, my aim is to use feminist new materialism to upset the repetitive partition between violence and symbolic activities. Throughout, I suggest that, instead of focusing on talk *about* violence, organizations, individuals, and groups that want to intervene in rape should focus on how violence communicates, that is, how violence emerges through continuous material–discursive intra-actions.

This shift—focusing less on talk about violence and more on how violence communicates—is grounded in feminist new materialism. It requires reconceptualizing what scholars call the "objective referent," the thing that exists in the world. In prevailing intellectual traditions, a table—that object with a smooth, level surface and four legs that people sit around when they eat meals—is an objective referent. The word used to describe it (e.g., "table" in English or "mesa" in Spanish) is the reference, the symbol that corresponds to the object. This understanding of the objective referent is predicated upon the same split that separates talk from violence: Things simply exist, and researchers explain them in ways that remove or account for subjective observation.

Occasionally, this understanding comes into crisis, as it did in the early 20th century when scientists were studying light. They noticed that light sometimes appeared to be a particle, but at other times it appeared to be a wave. Under the word/world split, these results presented scientists with a serious problem. Per the accepted worldview at the time, light could not be two different things: It had to be either wave or particle, but not both. It seemed the experiments had produced inaccurate representations of light, the objective referent. Another interpretation of the results was possible: The prevailing understanding of the relationship between objective referent and reference was inaccurate. This alternative interpretation is a core principle for feminist new materialism. In Barad's (2007) iteration of the theory, she relied on Niels Bohr to argue that the objective referent—light, in this example—and observation—the particular conditions and apparatuses used to study it—are intertwined. In other words, what truly exists in the world (ontology) and how that world is known (epistemology) are inseparable. Per this feminist new materialist set of assumptions, the goal of science is not to describe the objective referent, but to account for the "intra-active objective referent," the material–discursive processes through which phenomena emerge (Barad, 1998).

In this chapter, to account for rape as an intra-active objective referent, I trace Title IX processes at universities in the United States. I focus, in particular, on federal guidance requiring certain members of universities to report sexual assaults. By concentrating on the laws, policies, and talk that surround these reporting requirements, I show some of the problems that arise when organizations adopt the representationalist approach to communication that I described in the last chapter. I illustrate the complex, material–discursive intra-actions through which those reports emerge, and I assert universities' reporting processes—one organizational way to talk about rape—are part of the broader system through which assault emerges. That is, university reporting processes are not separate from sexual violence. This reframing situates the organization as part of the phenomenon of rape, not simply the site at which it occurs. It is the grounds upon which I assert that violence communicates.

The title of this chapter suggests not only that violence communicates, but also that it communicates differently. Though violence is unlikely to present itself in neatly correspondent accounts, it still communicates. To notice that kind of communication requires moving outside the paradigm of representation. Feminist new materialists do so through diffraction, a process, method, and metaphor indebted to "a thick legacy of feminist theorizing about difference" (Barad, 2014, p. 168). Diffraction occurs when light encounters obstacles, and the light changes in that process of encounter. So, for example, when light from the moon encounters water in the earth's atmosphere, that encounter impacts the light. When people look up at the moon at night, they may see the effects of that process, but they will not see the process of diffraction itself. The moon will sometimes appear to have rings around it, and some of those rings are brighter than others. The variation in brightness happens because as light waves diffract, they interfere with one another, a process that either amplifies or diminishes the light.

Feminist new materialists have adapted this process as a metaphor and method for their projects. As she moved away from the representationalist paradigm, Haraway (1992) wanted to reclaim visual metaphors in ways that did not replicate "the same" elsewhere. She argued that difference emerges in a process akin to the one in which light meets water droplets in the atmosphere. Though difference may not be immediately observable, its effects are. Accordingly, when feminists participate in diffraction, they do not describe or reflect difference itself. In Haraway's (1992) words, they do not "map where differences appear, but rather [map] where the effects of difference appear" (p. 300). Diffraction makes evident the patterns that result from the encounters through which difference emerges.

Although feminist new materialism is routinely taken up in organization studies without attention to difference (e.g., Leonardi, 2013; Mutch, 2013), all writers who explicitly discuss diffraction make difference central (e.g., Barad, 2007; Haraway, 1997; Kaiser & Thiele, 2014; Sehgal, 2014). As the chapter proceeds, I participate in diffraction. I show a pattern that is a record of "the history of interaction, interference, reinforcement, difference" (Haraway, 1997, p. 273). I map not only the material–discursive intra-actions involved in reporting rape, but also how the effects of difference are evident in that system.

Communicating about violence? The insufficiency of representing rape

The trouble with representationalist approaches to campus rape started long ago, and it often shows up in debates over the prevalence of sexual assault. In the late 1970s, scholars found that few women had experienced rape (Koss et al., 2007). Their studies relied on survey questions that asked women, "Have you been raped?" Most participants answered "no," they had not been. If a word such as "rape" simply does or does not match an experience, then survey questions like this one can provide a good measure of how often assault happens.

But as they developed their measures during the 1980s, researchers recognized that many women answered questions about behavioral descriptions of rape differently. Participants who said they had not been raped often stated they had been forced to have sex (Fisher, 2009). To explain this apparent contradiction, many scholars argued the label "rape" is difficult to apply because violence is so normalized that it is hard to recognize, and victims are routinely blamed for assaults (Hamby & Koss, 2003). In this context, participants coped with internalized stigma around sexual assault by not identifying their own experiences of rape as such.

As I have shown in my own research on how people name experiences of sexual violence, the label "rape" does not merely describe a violent incident (K. L. Harris, 2011). It also impacts how people evaluate an individual's character as well as who people are to themselves and each other. For example, many women I interviewed were reluctant to describe their assaults as rapes because to use that word required them to see a person they loved as a rapist, not a caring partner. That shift in perspective, they argued, did not fit well with the ongoing, long-term relationships many of them had with the person who assaulted them. Moreover, using the label would also mean acknowledging themselves as victims of violence, and that acknowledgment would mean their own sense of identity had to change. When people wrestle with what to call an experience that meets legal definitions of rape, more is at stake than merely naming events in the world. Questions about identity, credibility, security, and morality are tangled in words that ostensibly only describe assault.

To develop accurate and valid measures of sexual violence prevalence is important, and researchers have done so (e.g., Koss et al., 2007). Any robust dialogue about a social problem can and should invite questions about numbers, how they are generated, and the many factors that shape those representations of violence. But the political climate in the United States makes the difficulties that accompany all rigorous research—including developing comprehensive descriptions of the world—even more complex for research on rape. As I write this book, the prevalence of sexual assault is hotly contested in public arenas. Indeed, high-ranking U.S. government officials—including powerful people in the justice system—deny that assault is assault. If we assume numbers and words simply represent the world, we overlook that these public squabbles are actually struggles over whose bodies are valuable and who has access to resources, including education. Public discourse about rape is embroiled in this mess.

In numerous mainstream media outlets, some groups' efforts to retain unearned privileges masquerade as debates about facts. This dynamic is most evident when public commentators claim statistics about campus sexual violence rates are false. The author of an opinion piece in the *Washington Post* made one of these arguments. George Will (2014) asserted many incidents of assault are just evidence of the "ambiguities of hookup culture" (para. 4). To illustrate these ambiguities, he described a woman who did not consent to sex. In a display of maddeningly artful circularity, Will used this clear case of rape to argue that rape is not, in fact, rape. The same month, in a similarly flawed attempt to debunk existing research, Christina Hoff Sommers argued women who say they have experienced rape make "exaggerated claims about intimacy" (Malmsheimer, 2014, para. 3). Academic research shows the opposite is true: The vast majority of young women who experience rape never name it as such (Orchowski, Untied, & Gidycz, 2013). Yet both Will and Sommers charged that academic prevalence studies are inaccurate because the people who experience these events overstate or mislabel what happened. Both pundits' allegations are predicated on the idea that numbers and words only represent what happens in the world accurately or not.

The word–world divide that animates their skepticism is also clear in attempts to rebut not only participants' understandings of the world, but also researchers' methods. In a piece titled "No, 1 in 5 women have not been raped on college campuses," *Washington Examiner* writer Schow (2014) argued that the oft-cited statistic is inaccurate because it differs based on how researchers word their survey questions. In all research, findings depend on measurement. Scholars spend years learning how to develop good measures and make claims far more nuanced than "this is the absolute number of women who experience rape on U.S. college campuses." To claim that statistics are inaccurate— and should be discarded—because results vary by measurement ignores how research becomes meaningful and how knowledge claims accumulate. If we adopt Schow's assumption that statistics are accurate only if all measures yield the same results, we have to discard the entire practice of developing statistics along with the results of that practice. More importantly, we also have to assume that language is disconnected from the world of hard facts, events, bodies, and objects. We have to hold the two apart.

These attempts to challenge sexual assault prevalence studies mimic the reasoning associated with the correspondent approach to communication that I outlined in Chapter 2. As I noted, Barad (2003) called this reasoning "representationalism." She said:

Representationalism is the belief in the ontological distinction between representations and that which they purport to represent; in particular, that which is represented is held to be independent of all practices of representing. That is, there are assumed to be two distinct and independent kinds of entities—representations and entities to be represented. . . . This taken-for-granted ontological gap generates questions of the accuracy of representations. For example, does scientific knowledge accurately represent an independently existing reality? Does language accurately represent its referent? (p. 804)

The author, Schow, whom I mentioned in the last paragraph, discarded knowledge about rape based on a (misguided) "no" answer to the first question about whether science represents reality correctly. Similarly, Will and Sommers discarded knowledge about rape based on their (uninformed) "no" answer to the second question about whether language represents the referent correctly. When people get caught up in questions of representation—and its accuracy—they miss some of the specific complexities around violence and its relationship to communication.

Representationalism does not only derail anti-rape activism. The same ideas also operate in the work of those who fight sexual violence. In 2014, 91% of about 11,000 U.S. colleges reported zero rapes (Becker, 2015b). Assessing these numbers, Lisa Maatz from the American Association of University Women reflected, "The data reported by the nation's colleges simply defy reality" (Becker, 2015a, para. 2). Maatz is right that the reports required by federal law generate inaccurate numbers, and experts know something about why. People who experience sexual violence tend not to disclose those experiences to formal sources such as police or school officials (Orchowski & Gidycz, 2015; Starzynski, Ullman, Filipas, & Townsend, 2005). Additionally, complex gendered/raced/sexualized discourses exclude some accounts of assault from being reported (K. L. Harris, 2017), and campuses intentionally and unintentionally underreport (Lombardi & Jones, 2009). Anti-rape activists and allies might rightly turn their attention to producing better numbers, but they might also pose different questions such that correspondence between rapes and reports cannot be higher education's primary concern about sexual violence.

Those of us invested in reducing and preventing rape might mistakenly assume that if only we can develop better counts of violence—better mirrors for the world that serve as evidence of assault—we can gain the traction needed to combat rape. This idea was at work in the development of the Clery Act. In 1986, Jeanne Clery was raped and murdered while she was a first-year student at Lehigh University. After Clery's death, her parents advocated for more accessible and transparent information about campus assaults. The law, passed in 1990, now requires campuses to track statistics for certain crimes and, moreover, to disclose those statistics in an annual report. Part of the rationale for the legislation was that if Clery's parents had known about rates of violence at Lehigh, they would never have sent Clery to study there, and she would still be alive. The law is predicated on the idea that representations of the world can enhance safety. Transparency, disclosure, and more information are thought to yield choices that help people to avoid violence. By this logic, numbers and other symbols tell us something about the world yet remain apart from it.

If definitive representations of assault could shift a culture of violence—as the Clery Act's rationale implies—I would expect that people would take those representations seriously. Yet even when talk about violence is obviously connected to real-world events, people routinely dismiss it. We can see how this resistance to representation operates in a case at the University of Colorado that unfolded prior to and during 2013. At one department's social event, a male graduate student repeatedly put his hands on a female graduate student's breast and genitals. A university investigator found that the assailant did not violate any university policy, despite two voicemails the assailant left for the woman in which he acknowledged committing the assault and apologized for his actions. The university's investigative report included information about how hard the assailant had worked in his field, how close he and his wife were, and his Catholicism. These details were irrelevant to whether the assault happened, and the investigation also relied on other extraneous information. The investigator wrote in the official report, "I asked Respondent if he finds Complainant attractive. He said no, and that he is attracted to women who are physically similar to his wife. Respondent's wife and Complainant are physically dissimilar" ("How a perpetrator," 2013, para. 23). In this statement, the investigator implied not only that the assailant had good character, but also that he would not have assaulted the female graduate student because he was not attracted to her. The investigative report writer mistakenly assumed that sexual desire alone—not power and dominance—motivate assault. Furthermore, the investigator suggested that marriage, religious devotion, and academic credentials make it unlikely a person will be sexually violent. In this case, even the most direct reference to a crime—a statement like "I am sorry I assaulted you"—did not elicit appropriate responses to campus sexual violence.

Clear representations often do not lead people to acknowledge sexual assault and hold perpetrators accountable, and I offer one additional case as another example. In 2011, at Harvard, Kamilah Willingham filed a complaint on behalf of herself and a friend. A law student had assaulted both women. A university investigation found that the assailant "had initiated sexual contact with the complainant while she was asleep or unconscious, and not capable of consenting" and, furthermore, that the assailant had also "initiated sexual contact with the friend while she was incapable of consenting" (Harvard Law Administrative Board, 2011, p. 2). A grand jury, in separate criminal proceedings, indicted the assailant on two felony accounts of indecent assault and battery. Though the assailant was dismissed from the law program after these findings, he was later allowed to return to the school. After Willingham's story was featured in the documentary *The Hunting Ground*, 19 law professors at Harvard wrote a public letter criticizing Willingham's and the film's account. In it, they claimed, "There was never any evidence that [the assailant] used force" (Bartholet et al., 2015, p. 1). The professors misunderstood that sexual contact without consent *is* force. They further claimed that "there was insufficient evidence to support the charges made against [the assailant]" (Bartholet et al., 2015, p. 1). An argument about correspondence and representationalism—proof of rape that reflects an event in the world—was used to defer, deflect, and distort consideration of violence. In response to the letter the law professors penned, Willingham (2016) said back to them, "The message you're sending is clear: don't bother reporting unless you have a written confession, a witness, and—oh, wait, we had those things! This raises a great question, actually: What would it take for you to believe a sexual assault survivor?" (para. 10). As Willingham underscored, even clear evidence—a perpetrator saying, "I committed an assault," combined with eyewitness confirmation of the assault—did not prompt an acceptable response to sexual violence. The law professors discounted the assailant's admission of guilt *and* the eyewitness's account based on the premise that words—representational evidence—did not match the world.

A distinction between symbols and things in the world supports the illusion that people can simply talk about violence, and that illusion depends on an understanding of the violence–communication relationship that lacks nuance. The persistent bifurcation of discourse and materiality results in a predictable set of public debates: Is what experts know accurate? Will people stop discounting rape if they receive more complete representations? In the case of sexual violence on college campuses, asking and answering these questions does not prompt sufficient organizational interventions. On the contrary, the assumption that word and world are separate often supports inappropriate or nonexistent responses to rape. Those of us who want to end rape should not stop insisting that people take clear evidence and proof of assault seriously. We also should not stop counting, conducting prevalence studies, or using representationalist accounts of violence. But we also need an additional strategy and understanding of the world. If we interrupt the fissure between word and world rather than continue only to assert the validity and accuracy of our claims, it is harder to dismiss the inextricable links between symbolic and material systems. Representationalism must not continue to set the terms of the conversation.

Describing Butler's *Bodies That Matter*, Kirby (1997) suggested that, even as Butler pushed back on the feminization of matter, she simultaneously rendered "the materiality of matter . . . unspeakable . . . for the only thing that can be known about it is that it exceeds representation" (p. 108). People often make similar claims about violence: It defies representation and (therefore) cannot speak. In this section, I have problematized the idea that rape is simply represented (or not) in reports of sexual assault. I have also suggested that the representationalist paradigm produces inadequate responses to sexual violence. When organizations require neat correspondence to drive their decision-making, their resulting interventions fail because they overlook how violence communicates.

In the next section, I continue to develop my argument by shifting the focus away from talk about rape. Feminist new materialists have argued that one cannot stand apart from the world and simply tally its contents. Instead, any measurement is inextricably bound up in the phenomenon under study. As I move forward, instead of meditating on how accurately scholars and organizations count instances of rape, I focus on how violence communicates. More specifically, I trace some of the material–discursive processes through which rape becomes intelligible at U.S. universities. In so doing, I move toward conceptualizing sexual violence as an intra-active objective referent.

How violence communicates: Toward an intra-active objective referent

Violence communicates not via representation, but through material–discursive processes. It is a phenomenon that "can be recognized only insofar as the conditions of its emergence are made explicit" (Fraser, 2002, p. 615). To trace some of these conditions, I describe a study I conducted at one university, the pseudonymous Public Research University (PRU). I focused on mandatory reporting of sexual violence, one mechanism universities use to generate numbers of assaults, as required by federal law. As the section proceeds, I detail the complex and continuous intra-actions surrounding the reporting process at this university. My argument is not that reports are inaccurate, false, or undercounted. Instead, I concentrate on the myriad processes that influence how rape becomes intelligible through mandatory reporting and, in so doing, build the claim that violence communicates.

When I designed the study and completed it, I was a member of PRU. I was also considered a "supervisor," a person responsible for making reports of sexual assault under the university's Title IX policies. I planned to interview PRU members about their experiences with reporting, and I was unsure whether I would be required to make reports if I learned about assaults during those interviews. If the reporting obligations applied in this context, I needed to think through potential ethical conflicts between the multiple communities to which I belonged. For example, as a feminist researcher and expert in trauma, I wanted participants who experienced violence to retain control over what happened if they disclosed those experiences. If I was required to make reports based on what they told me, I might revictimize participants. Yet as a member of PRU, not to report would neglect some of my responsibilities as an employee. Furthermore, it would contribute to the undercounting of assault in the university's official numbers. Those numbers were used to persuade administrators that campus programs needed more resources for sexual assault prevention. Additional risks also existed. It was possible I would learn a participant had not complied with the university's reporting policy. If I was required to report information from that participant's interview, and if the university then learned the participant had not followed the reporting policy, that participant could be subject to university sanctions, including written reprimands, reduction in salary, or demotion.

Looking for ways to reduce risks to participants, I solicited advice from several university members who were responsible for implementing and enforcing mandated reporting. I asked about a clause in PRU's policy that exempted some supervisors from reporting if their professional or university responsibilities obligated them to withhold some information. For example, university ombudsmen were exempt from some reporting requirements. I suggested that, similarly, as a researcher, the ethical commitments associated with that role and formalized through the Institutional Review Board (IRB) required me to keep confidential what I learned about sexual assault during interviews on mandated reporting.

The people responsible for overseeing the policy argued that researchers did not qualify under this exemption, and they confirmed their perception with university counsel. They explained that PRU members who qualified under this exception had legally established confidentiality: therapist–client privilege in the case of psychologists and counselors and attorney–client privilege for lawyers. They said the same legal precedent for confidentiality did not exist for researcher–participant relationships. I spent nearly a year at PRU in back-and-forth conversation with the IRB and the offices that oversaw Title IX pointing out potential problems and brainstorming possible solutions. The IRB recommended I conduct an anonymous online survey rather than speak to people during face-to-face interviews. This design was not a good option for my goals, and it did not fit with the assumptions I was making about knowledge production. At one point, in frustration, I mentioned to the Title IX office that, ironically, a policy designed to produce more knowledge about sexual violence on campus was limiting the studies that could be conducted to complement knowledge derived from reporting.

The American Association of University Professors (AAUP)—an advocacy group for academic freedom and tenure—articulated concerns about scenarios like this one. They argued, "Even before reaching the publication stage, scholars may find their research processes stymied, as Institutional Review Board (IRB) protocols that previously protected the confidentiality of study participants as an ethical obligation are overruled by administrators who interpret such rights as conflicting with Title IX reporting guidelines" (Lieberwitz et al., 2016, p. 55). Their worry played out in my case. The AAUP concluded this kind of incident indicates Title IX threatens academic freedom and principles of shared governance. I do not agree with that claim because—as I explain below—the problem is not Title IX. The description of my process should not be read as support for the AAUP's concern. Instead, I use this discussion about the complexities of designing this study to launch the argument I continue to develop: Violence communicates through continuous material–discursive intra-actions, and these continuous intra-actions organize rape.

Faculty Against Rape (2016)—a group of U.S. scholars dedicated to addressing sexual violence—noted that, contrary to the AAUP's criticism, the actual requirements of Title IX do not threaten academic freedom. Unfortunately, the actual requirements—and their implications for research—have not always been clear. Years after I designed the study, the Office for Civil Rights issued guidance explicitly detailing that exceptions to mandated reporting, like the one I requested at PRU, are permitted under Title IX. Additionally, the Prevention Innovations Research Center at the University of New Hampshire published a white paper outlining the legal precedent that exempts researchers from varied reporting requirements (Potter & Edwards, 2015). At the time I designed the study, these documents had not been published, and the PRU decision-makers with whom I interacted were likely unaware that Title IX does not require researchers to sacrifice participant confidentiality. My efforts to launch the study show that research designed to provide one kind of evidence about sexual assault was already embedded in a skein of laws, ethical communities, bureaucracy, policy, text, influence, and power, even before it began. As such, both the reporting process *and* my study of it are embedded in the material–discursive intra-actions around rape. They are both part of the phenomenon of sexual violence.

The same tangle of factors at work in the study design also shaped what was and could be said during interviews for my study. Since it seemed unlikely I would be able to convince decision-makers at PRU that I should be exempt from reporting information I learned during research interviews, I pursued other solutions. Based on advice from both the IRB and the Title IX offices, I told participants I would not ask them about specific incidents of sexual violence. Additionally, I mentioned that if they wanted to discuss specific incidents, I might need to make a report. If they wanted me to make a report, I would do so. I let them know that if they did not want me to make a report, they should omit people's names, locations of incidents, and dates of assaults. Without those specific details, it would be unlikely I would need to make a report. As a result of these parameters, if participants and I wanted to discuss sexual violence and *not* make reports, we also could not make statements that would directly correlate to objects, people, and events in the world. We had to avoid representationalism. To talk about violence and protect confidentiality, we had to discuss violence in abstract, generalized terms. We could not, if we wished to avoid systems that could eliminate participants' control over their own stories, simply name names and give dates, items often considered to be most representationalist.

Because of these complexities, participants and I spoke at length before and during interviews about how to navigate our various roles. We often paused in the middle of our discussion to further clarify with each other what we should and should not say. Frequently, participants made explicit comments about the omissions in our discussion. Comments like Rachel's are characteristic of these qualifiers: "I can speak to the questions so I'm not breaking confidentiality and providing identifying information. So I'll try—so this might be somewhat abstract." In this comment, Rachel acknowledged that her statements were unlikely to seem like correspondent accounts, like representations of things that had happened. Her comment emerged from the layers of negotiation surrounding the study, including my own interactions with IRB and Title IX offices as well as federal guidance. The possibility of direct reference, or unmediated representation, crumbled under this set of conditions. Reporting procedures designed to produce representations of sexual violence led, in many instances in this study, to people avoiding those representations. Though direct representational evidence of rape was not present in the conversations I had, violence still communicated. Statements like Rachel's were evidence of the effects of an encounter among incidents of rape, the reporting system, and the many other material–discursive intra-actions that make up the phenomenon of sexual violence. Rachel's comments do not constitute communication about violence. Instead, they are part of the nonrepresentational mode through which violence communicates.

Similar evidence of the effects of material–discursive intra-actions is notable elsewhere in participant comments. Many people who did not agree to participate in the study made statements like these: "I don't think I would tell you if I hadn't followed the reporting policy" or "I don't think I'd be willing to participate in your study knowing what I know now." In remarks like these, people suggested that what they would or could say fit uncomfortably—or not at all—within the factors that shaped the study. They may have been concerned about how to navigate reporting requirements, may have been interested in protecting the interests of assault survivors, or may have knowingly or un-knowingly violated their responsibility to make reports of assault. These fears—and the details those people who did not enroll might have shared—are not absent. This "missing" information is not neatly packaged in correspondent data in which people speak in depth *about* their concerns, but nevertheless it communicates and becomes intelligible as I trace the material–discursive intra-actions through which this study and book emerged.

People's fear about how to navigate reporting requirements, and their awareness of possible negative consequences for speaking about those requirements, also shaped my conversations with those individuals who agreed to be interviewed. Two participants asked not to be recorded because they felt uncomfortable about the risk of being identified. In a clear moment where a participant reflected upon her hesitation and reluctance to speak openly about mandatory reporting at the university, Pat said this:

> Pat: I mean, I think it's—to be as honest as I was about the interview, I'll admit there's a little bit of, like, "I just told exactly what I thought" [laughs]. You know what I mean?
>
> Kate: A little hesitation about that?
>
> Pat: Mmm-hmm.
>
> Kate: Do you want me to turn this [the recorder] off, by the way?
>
> Pat: No, I mean—
>
> Kate: Okay.
>
> Pat: —I've already said the damaging things. But . . .
>
> Kate: So, like, a hesitation around being critical about the way things are happening here?
>
> Pat: Yeah. Mmm-hmm.
>
> Kate: Yeah. And, like, a sense of . . .
>
> Pat: Just 'cause, like, "What if somebody got a hold of this [recording] and then"—'cause that's [PRU], right? I mean that's just—Even though I'm intimately involved with, like, working on this for campus and things like that.

In this excerpt, Pat alluded to a concern that by speaking openly and critically about mandatory reporting she could incur negative consequences. She expressed this sentiment most directly in her question, "What if somebody got a hold of this?" Our conversation was connected to PRU's policy, the recording equipment, already existing interactions at PRU, imagined future loss of social and economic capital, and fears about how documented statements can be taken out of context. Pat's comments, like other details in this section, illustrate the organization of sexual violence. They are interesting not primarily because they show that what people say is influenced by both material and discursive factors. This claim is well established in feminist work. Instead, Pat's comments are important because they are part of the phenomenon of sexual violence making itself intelligible. The statements she did and did not make are both part of how violence communicates.

In this section, I shifted away from understanding rape as an event that can be represented to understanding sexual violence as a phenomenon that is continually organized through complex material–discursive intra-actions. Under this feminist new materialist and communicative approach, talking about rape is not the sole way to know about rape. Instead, rape communicates through the complex and ongoing intra-actions among rape, reporting, and myriad other processes at PRU. Fraser (2002) issued some cautions about understanding an objective referent to be intra-active:

> This is not to say that the object is the product of . . . observation (or . . . that matter is the product of discourse), nor that the object is observation-independent (as in classical realism), nor even that it is not the object that is "really" being observed because its materiality is . . . inaccessible to language. (p. 614)

When applied to sexual violence, Fraser's comments suggest several implications of understanding rape from a feminist new materialist perspective: (a) Rape does not require someone to represent it for it to exist, and when people speak about their experiences of assault they are not speaking fictions into being; (b) Rape and discourse are interdependent, even though the physicality of assault cannot be denied; and (c) Though rape and other forms of sexual violence may sometimes be unspeakable, shrouded in silence, or impossible to talk about, they nevertheless communicate.

This shift toward understanding sexual violence as a material–discursive phenomenon—as an intra-active objective referent—challenges representationalism. It highlights the complex, diffuse processes through which rape becomes intelligible to other parts of the world. These intra-actions are part of how violence communicates. When rape is an intra-active objective referent, ways of knowing it are not entirely distinct from it. On the contrary, "knowledge-making practices . . . are material elements that contribute to, and are part of, the phenomena we describe" (Barad, 2007, p. 32). The reporting process is not separate from assault, nor is my study of the reporting process. Rape, reporting, and this book are all part of the phenomenon of sexual violence. In the next section, I continue participating in diffraction, and I turn my attention more explicitly to difference. I detail how evidence of its effects show up in the material–discursive intra-actions through which rape organizes.

How violence communicates: Mapping the effects of difference

When rape is conceptualized as an intra-active objective referent, it cannot be observed (or represented) directly. Although representations of it are not available, evidence exists of the effects of the material–discursive entanglements of sexual violence. In this section, some of that evidence emerges. I map the effects of difference in the reporting process. Furthermore, I suggest that when organizations rely solely on a representationalist approach to communication, they miss how violence communicates because they can ignore or discount these effects of difference.

In analyses of the data from the original study, I showed that individuals at the intersections of marginalized racial and gendered groups were less likely to disclose about their experiences of sexual violence. They were also less likely to have control over the disclosures they did make. Mandated reporters at the intersections of marginalized groups were also more likely to hear other PRU members make disclosures to them about sexual violence. Additionally, those same mandated reporters were more likely to understand disclosures of sexual assault to be reportable, and thus they were more likely to make reports and incur the associated risks (K. L. Harris, 2017).

Women, in particular, were explicitly discouraged from making reports. Study participant Meg, who was a professional at PRU, relayed a troubling story. In her office, other professional staff repeatedly flirted with undergraduate female staff and made inappropriate statements to them. Based on her supervisor's recommendation, Meg called the Title IX office to make several reports about these incidents. The Title IX investigator who answered the phone remarked that Meg called the Title IX office too often and was reporting too much. Meg told me that the Title IX office later apologized for those comments. Nonetheless, Meg says the investigator's suggestion that she overreported left her with a lasting negative impression.

Meg said the investigator was explicitly discouraging her from making reports and questioning her credibility. Meg and I discussed her impression that the investigator's response was based, in part, on sexist stereotypes that women are hypersensitive and overreact to unimportant incidents. Although reporting is required when sexual harassment occurs, the person who received Meg's call seemed to hope that people would not actually make reports of every incident of harassment. Per Meg's account, the complex gender systems that lead people to doubt women's accounts of the world were playing out when she made phone calls to the reporting office. In her story, the effects of difference are evident.

The effects of raced and gendered difference surrounding reporting also came up at some meetings I attended at PRU. After several hate crimes on PRU's campus, students organized a series of dialogues for PRU members to discuss racial–gender discrimination, harassment, and assault at the school. At the beginning of the second meeting I attended, a group of undergraduate students walked single-file into the room. Most protestors were students of color, LGBTQ people, and advocates and allies for underrepresented campus populations. A spokesperson said they had been asked to explain themselves repeatedly, but the university ignored their testimonies about violence at PRU. One of the protestors, who identified herself as a recent graduate and a Latina, said that administrators claimed to be unable to "find the numbers" to substantiate students' claims. She retorted, "Of course! That would be terrible. Hate crimes happen every day." Her statements echoed Meg's observation that many PRU members are generally unwilling to acknowledge—or perhaps unable to bear witness to—the extent of sexual/racial violence at PRU.

By the recent graduate's account, administrators did not consider repeated testimonies as adequate evidence of a problem. Instead, they insisted on the necessity of a count, a particular representation of sexual–racial–gender violence. Her comment that hate crimes happen every day reveals one of the problems with trying to represent this kind of violence: Assault seems unremarkable for those who are insulated from it. Her statements resonate with what Kendall (2013) said about privilege and oppression: To ask people in power to notice the effects of systemic racial–gender differences is "like asking fish to notice water or birds to discuss air. For those who have privileges based on race, gender, class, religion, physical ability, sexual orientation, or age, it just is—it's normal" (p. 22). Representation of violence at PRU is similarly shaped by privilege and oppression: Reporting violence requires the fish (some mandated reporters) to see the water (sexual violence). This incident is evidence of the effects of difference in the phenomenon of sexual violence, one that includes material–discursive intra-actions surrounding reporting.

These effects of difference came up again in comments from Vin, an advocate for underrepresented students on PRU's campus. He explained that white members of the college routinely do not understand what they witness and hear about. He said that underrepresented students—many of whom are also mandated reporters—are more likely to identify reportable incidents of sexual violence. Further, because privilege protects white students from the same understanding, underrepresented students do extra labor to explain why something is reportable. Vin said this:

It seems like with the white counterparts—white students— it's a normal thing . . . *not* to report. . . . "Oh yeah, he did this and this. That's just what they do." You know, versus where a student of color has said, "They've done this and this." Almost pretty much the same type of action or behavior, and they report that out. Maybe that's a cultural difference or a class difference. I don't know. It's interesting to see the same action or behavior and one group of folks, specifically our students of color, report that out versus our white counterparts where it's like, "Oh, that's just normal." See, that's not right. . . . Even with our GLBT students who say, "Oh, this fraternity— this student called me out because I was identified as GLBT and they said this and that." And they, our GLBT students who are underrepresented on this campus, they report it out too. But they are also white students as well. So it's just different. . . . It feels like the white students are just thinking it's a normal behavior and it's not.

Vin suggested that, for privileged students associated with whiteness, many descriptions of reportable instances seem ordinary and unremarkable. Vin pointed out that two individuals can provide identical descriptions or representations of an incident and still understand what happened differently. Vin suggested that the difference depends on the material–discursive systems surrounding privilege. People most associated with whiteness, heterosexuality, and wealth are least likely to recognize sexual violence and thus least likely to make the required third-party report. In contrast, those PRU members at the intersections of underrepresented social groups—including race, sexuality, class, and gender categories—are more likely to understand some behavior as problematic. As a consequence, PRU's reports of assault are low because people most associated with privilege shield PRU from having more complete counts.

Vin's comments exemplify a theme that appeared across the data for the study at PRU, one that particularly resonated with peers I consulted who are mandated reporters at other institutions. Every interview participant but one alluded to the possibility that reporters may not recognize when another PRU member is talking about a reportable incident of sexual violence. For example, they suggested that if a male student at PRU said, "I was out last night and said no but he kept going with sex anyway," many PRU mandated reporters would not interpret that statement as a description of rape. In each of the mandatory reporting training sessions I observed, the trainer mentioned that people who speak about their experiences of rape, sexual assault, harassment, or discrimination are unlikely to label them explicitly. In these meetings, PRU officials acknowledged that when people speak about sexual violence, other people must interpret what they say. But acknowledgment that a lifetime of experience in a group affects that interpretation was absent from policy documentation, training sessions, and my interviews with five enforcers of mandatory reporting. In other words, embodiment within social systems impacts the physical–symbolic circulation of violence, yet PRU does not address that aspect of systemic sexual violence. People who live in brown or feminine or queer or impoverished bodies exist in different relationships to violence than their more privileged counterparts, and the effects of those differences played out in Title IX reporting at PRU.

When I shared my findings, the effects of difference in the reporting process were evident again. After the study at PRU concluded, I circulated a white paper that detailed my analytic claims. I shared the white paper with a number of people at PRU, including a group of attorneys with Title IX expertise. In that document, I stated the vast majority of participants indicated the burden of third-party reporting was unevenly distributed across the university. The people who I interviewed said that white women, men and women of color, as well as nonbinary and queer people of all races shouldered a disproportionate amount of the labor. The team of lawyers considered this claim, compared it to their data, and said,

> An examination of university-tracked employment data associated with reporters of all cases indicates that approximately 80% of reporting witnesses identify as Caucasian, 55% of all reporting witnesses identify as female and 45% as male . . . Thus, while the small segment of the [PRU] population you interviewed may feel that members of marginalized intersectional identities shoulder a greater reporting burden, this may not, in fact, be statistically accurate; and [it] is a bold conclusion to make based on the perception of a few employees without any supporting demographic data.

The legal team refuted the claim from my white paper. Though they granted the claim could be true for the individuals

I interviewed, they challenged that the claim could apply to PRU as a whole. They suggested that without comprehensive demographic data—representative descriptions—my claims were suspect. Indeed, the legal team cited percentages from their own data that appeared to disprove participants' claims. Their response seemed to echo the protestors' characterization of university administrators at the racial and gender justice forum: The legal team also could not find the numbers to support my characterization of participants' claims.

Hearing and reading the team's responses, I felt frustrated. As I mentioned in the previous section, the systems surrounding the university's reporting process prevented me from conducting a study that could have found data the team would find more convincing. Yet the claims resulting from the study I *could* conduct were faulted for not operating under the representational standards that had eliminated the possibility of those descriptions. Nevertheless, the white paper, the legal team's reactions to it, and my reactions to the legal team surfaced an important convergence. The scholars I cited at the opening of the chapter argued that violence destroys people's capacity to create direct representations of it. Similarly, the university's system for reporting violence—that is, the process for assessing, knowing, and measuring violence—made it nearly impossible to generate numbers that would reflect how difference shaped that system. Though violence undermines representational modes of communication—and traditional methods for knowing violence—it still communicates. I tried to show in the white paper, and I am trying to show in this chapter, a record of patterns that evidence a different mode of communication, the mode through which violence communicates.

After some time passed, scholars at other institutions reviewed the claims in my white paper in a practice called "peer debriefing" (Spall, 1998). Given their expertise in quantitative methods, they recommended additional analysis of the numbers the legal team provided. With their guidance, I found—using a more representative approach—that the information the legal team cited in the above passage actually supported what study participants had said. When I compared the legal team's numbers to PRU's total demographics at the time of the study, I found that white women along with women and men of color *did* report more than their white male counterparts. For example, though 45% of people who made third-party reports were male, 53% of PRU's possible third-party reporters were male. The proportion of men making reports was lower than the proportion of men at the university who could make reports. If the burden of reporting had been shared evenly, then the two percentages would have matched. The legal team discounted this representation—a symbol of the world—even though it matched what participants had said about the uneven burden of reporting. By that point, both the team and I were defensive, and our relationship had become somewhat adversarial. I could not help but continue to hear the legal team's comment about the claims in the white paper, ones that had now been verified through representation: too bold.

In each of these examples—Meg's encounter with the Title IX office, the racial and gender justice forum protests, Vin's explanations of conditions at PRU, and my own interactions with the legal team—the effects of difference operate. They provide evidence of a pattern that emerges as rape, reporting, and other dynamics encounter one another and diffract. Further, they are part of the organization of sexual violence and part of how violence communicates. Though it is likely that PRU members understand and are impacted by the reporting system differently, that is not the primary claim this chapter evidences. Instead, the chapter provides evidence of and participates in diffraction, the material–discursive intra-actions through which violence communicates.

Earlier in the chapter, I mentioned physicists whose experiments on light generated a knowledge crisis. In some of their studies, they poured light through two slits in a wall. The reporting process at PRU is akin to those two slits. In the physicists' study, the slits were the mechanism used to determine some truth about light. At PRU, the reporting process is the mechanism used to establish some truth about rape. But in both situations, the mechanism used to establish truth is actually part of the phenomenon being studied. In the physicists' experiment, when light encountered the slit, the light was impacted by that encounter. Similarly, when rape encounters the reporting system, it is impacted not only by that encounter, but by the many other material–discursive encounters or intra-actions that surround both rape and reporting. The process through which rape and reports impact one another (i.e., diffraction) is not directly observable. Instead, evidence of the effects of difference that emerge from those intra-actions can be recorded. That evidence is akin to the rings of varied brightness that appear around the moon, ones that I described in my initial explanation of diffraction. This evidence and the processes through which it emerges are how violence communicates (differently).

In the original studies on light, the physicists' findings threw the truth about light into question. It seemed that two mutually exclusive truths existed. If the scientists had not shifted their understanding of the world and of truth, they might have deemed the whole experiment a failure and discarded it. Similarly, when administrators and other decision-makers at universities cannot find the numbers to describe rape and other forms of assault, they often abandon attempts to intervene and transform the organization. But some of the physicists who studied light, rather than abandon the project, eventually developed quantum physics, a field that undermines traditional subject/object distinctions and generates new insights about phenomena being studied. Feminist antiviolence activism and scholarship—that which is still emerging and that which has been emerging over decades—is making a similar shift. Collectively, we might come to a different understanding of violence, one in which violence communicates, even when representation fails us.

Violence communicates differently

Violence defies representationalist approaches to communication. If organizations go looking for correspondent accounts of rape, they may conclude that rape is nonexistent or silent. But if organizations instead look for the effects of difference, especially in processes connected to violence, they will find ample evidence of sexual violence. Though violence defies representation, it communicates through the effects of difference, and I have mapped some of them in the reporting process at PRU. Because violence communicates differently (i.e., it defies representation and makes itself known through the effects of difference), universities need to pose different questions to reorganize themselves against sexual violence. Organizations tend to ask: "Does violence happen here? If it does, how often does it happen? How will we know when it happens?" Instead of focusing on how to describe and count violence, organizations should ask this question: "How does violence communicate?"

Anti-rape activists and educators would also benefit if they shifted their framework. Many of the participants in the study ran into challenges similar to those I encountered with the legal team. Some people at PRU responded to those challenges by seeking a more accurate count of violence. They worked within the assumption that the word and world can be meaningfully separated. When they presented more accurate counts of rape and other sexual assaults, many of those PRU members found that those counts were dismissed. That happened, for example, when the investigator chastised Meg for making too many reports. Anti-rape students and educators at PRU also responded to the challenges by using stories to push back on representationalism, as the activists at the PRU racial and gender justice forum did. After hearing stories at that protest and many others, administrators still clung to representationalism and required the activists to provide names, dates, and locations before the university would take action against sexual violence. Both of these efforts to communicate about violence (i.e., to talk about it and describe it to the organization) met pushback. Because of this, I suggest that it would be useful for activists, educators, and organizational members who want to thwart sexual violence to reject the demands of representationalism. Anti-rape movements would do well to pay attention to how violence communicates and how it communicates differently.

For some readers, my communicative and feminist new materialist interest in explicating the conditions of a phenomenon's emergence—including the effects of difference—may sound a lot like some of the principles for good qualitative research. For many years, feminists have challenged the objectivity of accepted knowledge practices, and they have developed methodologies that problematize subject/object splits. For example, some feminist scholars routinely work toward what Harding (1995) dubbed "strong objectivity," the development of rigorous claims by accounting for—rather than eliminating—the subjectivity of any method. Even so, decades ago, Haraway (1997) pointed out that many of these techniques retain the split between word and world. To borrow the language of communication theorists, these techniques align with a correspondence approach in which high-quality research mirrors the world while research that lacks rigor distorts it. Because violence defies representation, these techniques fail for research on violence and trauma

(Harris & Fortney, 2017). Given this context, the methods and claims in this chapter should not be read as an attempt to map distortions in the reporting process so that those distortions can be corrected. Though reports are not accurate counts of sexual violence, I am not primarily concerned with these inaccuracies, and I do not think reporting processes should be expanded so they "capture" more complete information. Instead, working in concert with trauma studies, I begin from the premise that violence does not communicate via representation. The chapter is a sketch of the epistemological and ontological shifts needed to notice how violence communicates differently.

Sexual violence—like other kinds of trauma—changes communication. Neurobiologists suggested that when people experience trauma, the areas of the brain responsible for language shut down (Brewin, 2007). Other scholars, too, argued that violence—or more precisely the pain that often accompanies violence—"does not simply resist language but actively destroys it" (Scarry, 1985, p. 4). In both these claims, violence is opposed to "language." That term is different from what I mean by communication. To say that violence opposes language is not also to say that violence cannot communicate. Violence interrupts linear stories (Samuelson, 2011), and it dampens a person's capacity to synthesize details and sensory information (Jenkins, Langlais, Delis, & Cohen, 1998). Given these qualities, people should not expect simply to describe assaults or find symbols to stand in the place of rape, though the public assumes these representations are possible when they engage in debates over the prevalence of sexual assault. Trauma studies scholars generally agree that perfect representations of rape are impossible, and my fusion of feminist new materialism and communication theories establishes this complementary claim: Even if violence defies language or speech, it nevertheless communicates.

Asserting that violence communicates differently makes it impossible to understand organizations as mere sites at which individual humans commit assault. The claim reframes both violence and also who or what can communicate. If violence communicates, it does not reside and operate solely in the physical world. Violence does not utter words, so if communication is something violence can do, then communication cannot be synonymous with speech. Instead, if communication is a more complex symbolic and physical process that exceeds speech, communication is not limited to discrete humans. Communication becomes the ongoing process of material–discursive entanglement. Without this reframing, organizations might merely listen to people describe their experiences of rape and then pursue one human to punish. But this approach misses something important that a communicative and feminist new materialist account of rape surfaces: Trauma and violence are not solely local. They are not events, they are not bound to one segment of linear time, and their impacts are not visited only on individual bodies. Violence is organized. Its material–discursive intra-actions are woven through an organization's processes and systems.

The argument that violence is dispersed and distributed, not limited to a time-bound physical event, resonates with existing research from trauma studies. For example, if paramedics respond to a gunshot wound, though a bullet did not tear their body's flesh, their proximity to trauma often elicits emotional and neurochemical responses similar to those of the person whose body was shot. These responses are called vicarious trauma or secondary traumatic stress (Baird & Jenkins, 2003; Figley, 1995; Schauben & Frazier, 1995). Though the conscious mind can distinguish a description of rape from the direct experience of rape, the unconscious mind cannot always discern the difference (R. Campbell, 2002; Matthews & Goodman, 2013). The source and impact of violence—even at the physiological level—is not well assessed by concentrating on a single human's experience of assault or by limiting the term "violence" to a moment of bodily injury. A feminist new materialist focus on communication—continuous material–discursive intra-actions—encourages broader thinking.

In politicized battles over numbers—and also in rigorous and important debates among researchers—people persistently avoid the idea that violence resides in intertwined physical and symbolic systems. Debates on the left, on the right, among scholars and laypeople, among feminists and misogynists are often animated by the idea that people can speak about violence, but not that violence itself communicates. Much of the apparatus for responding to and preventing sexual violence on college campuses in the United States relies on the idea that numbers can say something about what's going on, that reports based on survivors' disclosures of violent events can motivate change. And yes, to some extent they can. But if colleges stop there, they miss an opportunity to make more systemic changes and to focus on the organization of sexual violence. Feminists have long acknowledged that sexual violence involves both material and discursive factors, and a communicative, feminist new materialist approach helps to conceptualize these factors as intra-active, not distinct. Under this framework, violence cannot be conceptualized as silent. Instead, violence is a phenomenon embedded in the organization, one continually organized through material–discursive intra-actions that implicate systems of difference, including gender, race, and sexuality. Understanding violence in this way turns attention to the organizing that lies beyond the rapist.

Conclusion

Hekman (2008) said, "At the root of modernism is an absolute distinction between objective reality on the one hand and social construction on the other" (p. 91). Feminist new materialism unsettles this distinction; nature cannot meaningfully be separated from culture, object from subject, reason from emotion, body from mind, or physical from discursive. Although scholars are still in the process of eliciting that unsettling, it seems clear that a framework "that does not presuppose a gap between language and reality" is required (Hekman, 2008, p. 91). Violence—as a focal point for theory—provides an entrée into closing that presumed gap.

Violence is not easily represented. Nevertheless, a representationalist framework animates many organizational responses to violence. In the case of sexual violence, both a concern with numbers and an emphasis on reports operate within the paradigm of correspondence. Without challenges to that paradigm, the public, activists, and organizations alike remain embroiled in debates about what proof can conclusively demonstrate that rape and other forms of sexual assault are real, pervasive, defining aspects of higher education for many students and educators. When universities assume that reports under Title IX and the Clery Act represent violence, they grant those reporting processes an objective sheen. In the separation between reports and the world, they can miss the ways that whiteness, heteronormativity, and hegemonic masculinity shape Title IX, even as the law does important work. They can further miss that organizational reactions to violence—including those systems that report and measure it—are part of the ongoing phenomenon that organizes sexual violence.

This chapter has outlined part of what is at stake in a feminist new materialist turn. The assumption that talk corresponds to an independent reality motivates an endless search for proof of that reality. And yet, even when activist groups meet representationalist standards for evidence, society and individuals still discount that proof. The most clear and compelling representations become mired in complex processes attached to gender/sexuality/race. This happened with Meg's "over"-reporting, and it happened in the case of the University of Colorado graduate student whose assailant was excused based on his marriage and Catholicism. Seeing these kinds of failures, many feminists then rely on social construction. They show how people interpret representations through gendered lenses that presuppose women and other feminine bodies are hypersensitive and manipulative. But these constructivist stances end up failing too. They are subject to political jabs that misuse constructivist tenets in order to argue that everything is made up. That claim fits too conveniently with the idea that people who testify about being raped are liars who invent representations of the world and take pleasure in making false accusations.

Efforts to navigate these binds—these feminist dilemmas, as I have called them elsewhere (K. L. Harris, 2016a)—mark the emergence of feminist new materialism. Like all feminisms, new materialism is a political project. It is responsive to the peculiar demands that arise out of a sexist–racist world that needs to shift. It does not require reemphasizing the material: To do so would let the material remain apart from the discursive. Instead, it requires a mode of knowing and being that is neither constructivist nor realist, one that can theorize violence in ways that serve feminist politics.

To challenge the word/world split is risky. Feminist new materialism suggests that direct representation and description of assault is impossible. This suggestion could be problematic for feminist antiviolence work, especially that which depends upon facts about the world that stand on their own, separate from human bias. Haag (1999) made this point plain:

> Because the stakes are so high for women in their daily lives, feminists for decades have tried to nail down what violence is. The strategy has been to position a definition of violence beyond the vagaries of interpretation, where historically women's injuries and accounts of sexual violation often have been derided and systematically represented as indications of the woman's own licentiousness. In such an environment, it is only logical that feminism seeks after essences, unconditional properties . . . of violence, so that these cannot be misinterpreted or talked out of view. (p. xv)

Haag highlighted the risks associated with allowing the word and the world to mutually influence one another. When disbelief of rape and other violence is routine, some feminist political modes cling to representationalism and to fixed descriptions that cannot bend. Despite the harsh social and political climate in which this work occurs, I think the benefits of a feminist new materialist approach to violence outweigh these risks that Haag outlines. As I have argued in this chapter, no matter how persistent the efforts, feminists who fight rape will be unable to provide the "essences" and "unconditional properties" that representationalism demands. Violence defies them, so those of us who want to stop rape need a different way of understanding how violence communicates.

One other risk associated with this style of theorizing merits careful consideration, and it is at the center of the next chapter. Feminist new materialism challenges a clear line between human and nonhuman actors because that line has historically been implicated in sexism, racism, and other systems of oppression. Though feminist new materialism blurs the human/nonhuman split to upend oppressive systems, when the theory is used in proximity to violence, it could uphold those systems. In Chapter 4, I analyze how the human/nonhuman line functions at PRU. I pay particular attention to moments in which university members and actors assert that someone or something has the kind of agency that allows them to commit violence. The complex and paradoxical processes that govern those assertions are central to definitional struggles over violence, and they are deeply embedded in the systems of gender/race/sexuality that pattern the organization.

4

Agency organizes violence

Raced and gendered boundary-making practices for (non)human and discursive force

Scholars of organization—across organization studies, critical management, and organizational communication—have suggested that words (what some academics call discourse) have become too muscular (Alvesson & Kärreman, 2011; Carlile, Nicolini, Langley, & Tsoukas, 2013; Fleetwood, 2005), that a "constitutive view of discourse goes too far" (Ashcraft & Harris, 2014, p. 134). Promiscuous and slutty, social construction has given words a reputation for doing too much. Simultaneously, social construction is embattled against charges that it cannot account for objects, bodies, and aspects of the physical world. Harsher still, some argue that it reduces organization and all other phenomena to mere talk. Articulating this position, Reed (2005) argued that organizations, when approached through a constitutive view, end up with "no ontological status or epistemological significance beyond their textually created and mediated existence" (p. 1622). Everything organizational becomes mere words. This line of thinking is one animus for a material turn currently underway in studies of organizations, and scholars make that turn by paying more attention to the things and stuff of organizing—tables, bicycles, cameras, computers, and myriad other technologies.

These critiques of social construction are not unique to the subdiscipline of organizational communication. Feminist new materialists have passed similar judgment on a scholarly regime in which words make our worlds (e.g., Barad, 2007; Coole & Frost, 2010). Like some organizational scholars, feminists Alaimo and Hekman (2008) said that we need to "move beyond construction" (p. 6). Similarly, evaluating the implications of a "strong" social construction, Barad (2003) lamented, "Language matters. Discourse matters. Culture matters. There is an important sense in which the only thing that does not seem to matter anymore is matter" (p. 801). At surface, these feminist scholars' concerns about social construction and passive matter sound similar to organizational scholars' critiques. Despite the seeming resonance, feminist new materialists' critique of constitutive approaches has a different genealogy, one that consistently and carefully theorizes power and difference. In an interview with Dolphijn and van der Tuin (2012), Barad said, "I am not talking about . . . democratically distributing agency across an assemblage of humans and non-humans. . . . The notion of agency I am suggesting does not go against the crucial point of power imbalances" (p. 55). As Barad explained, feminist new materialists do not suggest that scholars simply focus on nonhuman agents in addition to human agents. To do so would not problematize the separation of human/nonhuman. Similarly, feminist new materialists do not want simply to minimize the bulging biceps of discourse. Instead, they suggest that words seem to bulk up when the category human—one routinely synonymous with agent—begins to encompass more of what it has traditionally left out. Accordingly, feminist new materialists want to problematize the categories "human," "nonhuman," and "agency" in relationship to gender/race/sexuality.

In the last chapter, I focused on how conceptualizations of communication shape definitional struggles over violence. In this chapter, I do the same for conceptualizations of agency. I trace what Barad (2007) called boundary-making practices, the "(re)-configurings of the world" that continuously animate perimeters around the (non)human (p. 140). I do so by interrogating "what gets left out . . . when agency is attributed to human or non-human entities and left at that" (Dolphijn & van der Tuin, 2012, p. 56). These exclusions have to do with power and difference. Contrary to critiques of strong social construction, I argue that discourse has not become uniformly too forceful. Instead, the capacities of discourse are uneven, and claims about its lack of force retrench gendered/raced violence. As I move forward, I argue that (a) gendered/raced/sexualized iterations of agency maintain the boundaries around "human" and "violence," and (b) these maintenance processes shape the organization's relationship to violence. Because of these dynamics, it is important for scholars who study organization to be attentive to difference as the field makes a material turn.

Race and gender pattern the exclusions of "human" and "agency"

Debates about agency—including those in the material turn—include questions about whether an entity (or network) that consists of more than one human can act. Though many organizational scholars take up this question in the abstract, they rarely consider it in connection to issues of race and gender (e.g., Leonardi, 2013; Robichaud & Cooren, 2013). Outside the discipline, however, these issues are extensively discussed. For example, Braidotti (2010), a feminist new materialist scholar, said explicitly that the "concept of 'the human' . . . has come to be identified with male, white, heterosexual, Christian, property-owning, standard-language-speaking citizens" (p. 208). Thus, when scholars consider nonhuman agency without also interrogating the category "human," they overlook complex and enduring power dynamics. Critical race scholars consistently point out that to consider the individual human as sole agent reinforces a racial status quo. Lawrence, Matsuda, Delgado, and Crenshaw (1993) described a racist hate incident on Stanford's campus in which two white students defaced posters, emblazoned them with racial slurs, and displayed them in a black dormitory. Many members of the predominantly white campus labeled the incidents as isolated, private acts committed by a few individuals and suggested the acts were disconnected from larger issues of climate. Yet as Lawrence et al. asserted, this framework was highly problematic: "This was injury to a group. To privatize it ignored the greatest part of the injury. The power of the poster's message was derived from its historical and cultural context . . . Without that context the defacement had no meaning" (pp. 8–9). In this passage, Lawrence et al. suggested that to frame the act as one committed by an individual, rather than an act embedded in an historical–cultural network of (non) human actors, was to overlook the very thing that made the act threatening, damaging, and violent.

Arguments like this one, which acknowledge that agency is intertwined with race, occur clearly and regularly in an extensive body of literature rarely read among organizational communication scholars (e.g., Carrington, 2017; Muñoz et al., 2015). For example, Jackson (2013) said that posthumanist theory's "acuity . . . was undercut when its scholars effectively sidestepped the analytical challenges posed by the categories of race, colonialism, and slavery" (p. 671). As she highlighted, theories of nonhuman action have challenged aspects of Enlightenment rationality while simultaneously retaining and amplifying whiteness and imperialism. These racial dynamics of agency are also linked with an ability to talk. Seshadri (2012) argued that speech is often used to distinguish people from other animals. She added that racism—a "practice of dehumanization" (p. ix)—creates boundaries around who or what is considered to have human qualities, including the ability to speak. Organizational communication has rarely attended to race (Ashcraft & Allen, 2003; Nkomo, 1992), and this absence makes it even more important that scholars in the field be attentive to the ways in which the conflation of agency and speech can operate in the service of white supremacy.

Critical race scholars have repeatedly demonstrated that the law has an uneven—and raced—understanding of the extent to which speech is agentic. For example, C. I. Harris (1993) showed how the law upholds whiteness when it protects reputation. Describing a case from 1957, she noted, "To call a white person 'Black' is to defame her. . . . The allegation was likely to cause injury. A Black person, however, could not sue for defamation if she was called 'white'" (pp. 1735–1736). Harris asserted that speech is not considered uniformly agentic. Instead, it is considered able to commit injury when it challenges white supremacy. In the case she discussed, an equation between whiteness, reputation, and property made only some kinds of agency intelligible. In contrast, when speech kept systemic racism in place, it was not ascribed a similar capacity to act and, consequently, to inflict harm.

Conceptualizations of agency are also linked to gendered power dynamics. Feminists have long noted this phenomenon, especially when they have theorized rape. In her discussion of the history of feminist antiviolence activism, Haag (1996) argued, "A certain homogenization of violence as a 'crime' of the powerful enables the feminist condemnation of 'violence' as an exercise of male, patriarchal traditions. Women, by these accounts, are presumptively 'available' for violation, and men presumptively capable of violating" (p. 47). She noted that when patriarchy is the conceptual framework for understanding sexual violence, masculinity becomes associated with violence, femininity with violation and victimization. MacKinnon (1989) noted a similar problem in pithier language: "Man fucks woman; subject verb object" (p. 124). In both examples, the ability to commit violence becomes synonymous with being a full human, while not committing violence makes a person merely a victimized object, not a human subject. Some have argued that, under this grammar, femininity— and thereby many women—is intelligible only in the absence of agency (e.g., Carillo Rowe, 2009). Feminists have noted that a capacity for violence seems to be a precursor for being an agent and, as a consequence, being considered human.

In sum, scholars outside of organizational communication have outlined in great detail the ways in which the problem of agency cannot be disconnected from the power dynamics associated with gender and race. To individualize agency— that is, to root it only in one human—is to disconnect it from the historical and cultural processes through which race and gender accrue meaning. Moreover, agency and speech have often collapsed, as have agency and violence, to exclude some people from being recognized as human. Barad (2007) noted that "the very practices by which the differential boundaries of the human and the nonhuman are drawn are always already implicated in particular materializations" (p. 153). I would add that violence is part of those materializations. In the analysis that follows, I show how some of these raced/gendered conceptualizations of agency—and the category "human"— play out at PRU.

Active discourse combats violence, but "inactive" discourse upholds the gendered and raced status quo: Organizing the uneven force of discourse

In this section, I show how gendered/raced dynamics shape PRU's understandings of the actions associated with reporting rape. I consider situations in which PRU members tell other PRU members about their experiences of sexual violence. Following many of these disclosures, the listener is obligated to make a report of the assault to the university's Title IX offices, and that report triggers the university's official responses to sexual violence. By analyzing contests over which parts of these conversations can and should be considered active, I build the argument that discourse is not uniformly too forceful or too agentic. On the contrary, in some instances, its capacity to impact the organization is limited. Whether these conversations are (in)active, muscular, or weak depends on complex processes connected to gendered/raced systems of power.

The struggle over the action/agency associated with disclosures of sexual violence routinely shows up when PRU members explain why the mandatory reporting system exists. When offering one such explanation, the person leading a training for faculty on Title IX processes said this: "If someone is coming to you, they are coming to you because they want it [the sexual violence] addressed." The trainer went on to explain that the university's mandatory reporting process ensures that the university addresses sexual violence when people disclose it, thus responding to the discloser's presumed wishes. PRU's online discrimination and harassment training offered a similar explanation when it suggested that PRU members talk to people at the university about the assaults they experience because they want the violence to stop. All five participants who were responsible for implementing and overseeing the mandatory obligation to report offered similar statements, and the same rationale was reiterated in most of the university trainings on sexual harassment that I attended. These explanations assume that a person's intent for disclosing a violent episode is instrumental, and, moreover, that disclosure solicits a particular kind of action separate from the disclosure itself. By repeatedly offering this rationale, PRU members position mandatory reporting as a mechanism that prompts appropriate action from the university. The disclosure and the report are not active, but the disclosure followed by a report is a catalyst for the university's active response.

The statement that people disclose their experiences of sexual violence in order to prompt a response from PRU is undoubtedly accurate in some cases. Many PRU members who speak about their experiences of harassment, rape, and other sexual violence may indeed be doing so because they want the organization to investigate, begin disciplinary procedures, and take other concrete actions. Yet this rationale overlooks other reasons why these conversations may happen and, in underemphasizing these other possibilities, sets aside ways in which disclosure itself is active. Researchers have shown that people share information about themselves for catharsis, self-clarification, self-validation, or reciprocity (Derlega & Grzelak, 1979). These reasons do not include prompting additional action from third parties. Indeed, some individuals at PRU may speak about their experiences of violence and not want a formal report to follow. Because disclosure has emotional and relational impacts, it could be considered active—or even an agent—in and of itself. But if talk is merely a means to an end, a way to describe the world in order to later impact it, disclosure does nothing by itself. To extricate action from disclosure in this way requires the word/world separation I troubled in the last chapter. PRU offers an explanation that repeatedly places action before and after the disclosure but not during it.

The assumption that people speak about experiences of sexual violence because they want to prompt an official response from the university is gendered. It depends upon masculine norms that evacuate action from speech. Tannen (2001) and Wood (2013), among others, argued that gender influences why people speak to one another. Per the tenets of genderlect theory, some people talk primarily to "report": As they speak, they demonstrate knowledge, solve problems, establish authority, and navigate rules. These people prioritize masculine uses of speech (but are not necessarily men). Other people talk primarily to establish "rapport": They talk to create mutually beneficial, equal relationships, and they are said to prioritize feminine uses of speech. Applying this framework to mandated reporting, the rationale that people speak about sexual violence because they want PRU to do something about it is associated with masculinity—with the assumption that people speak in order to solve problems. In short, this statement about the mandatory reporting obligation argues that disclosure is really for instrumental purposes, not for soliciting advice, support, and empathy alone. Disclosure is figured as a request for "report."

Although PRU's repeated suggestion that disclosure is inactive seems to align talk, femininity, and passivity, that equation does not always uphold the gendered status quo. Indeed, sometimes the assertion that talk is inactive challenges the gendered normativity that maintains systemic sexual violence. For instance, in a training session on PRU's Title IX practices, the training leader discussed Jerry Sandusky's repeated assaults of boys. These incidents occurred between 1994 and 2009 while Sandusky was associated with Pennsylvania State University. The incidents later propelled both him and Penn State into the U.S. national spotlight. Several people at the school were charged with obstructing justice and failing to report Sandusky's child abuse. The trainer at PRU said this about the Penn State scandal: "Why do we have that mandatory obligation to report? . . . Have you heard about Penn State? Lots of people knew about [the sexual assaults], lots of people talked about it. But talking about it doesn't ensure that the campus is safe." In this statement, talk is framed as an ineffective response to violence: It does not produce security and it does not stop assaults. By this logic, talk has limited capacity to produce concrete changes in the world. But the trainer is not suggesting that talk is always impotent. Instead, the trainer locates a particular kind of action that talk can take: It often supports the continuing organization of sexual violence.

In one of the interviews I conducted, one enforcer of PRU's mandated reporting, Emma, echoed this sentiment:

> Obviously you're familiar with Penn State. And I think, really, when we talk about the most important goal [of mandated reporting], it's to make sure that our culture is nowhere near those environments. It's nowhere near a culture where people are going to talk, if you will, but it's not ever going to be addressed. . . . It's one thing to talk, and at Penn State, I mean, there were a lot of people that knew. . . . *There was a lot of talking: rumors, chatter, and actual knowledge, both. And then nothing got done, for decades in one case*, you know, and so I think that really is the goal. The goal is to make sure that that is never where we come out. (emphasis added)

In these statements, Emma suggests that despite lots of talk, "nothing got done" at Penn State. She rightly points out that organizations can fail to respond appropriately—or even at all—to members' knowledge of wrongdoing, abuse, and assault. At surface, Emma's comments appear to reinforce a division between talking and acting. She appears to say that "a lot of talking" accomplished nothing. Organizational scholars who assume that talk is active might criticize Emma's assertion and instead root around for what the rumors and chatter accomplished. Indeed, in my own initial analysis of this interview, I saw only a problematic separation between discourse and doing. Upon additional readings, however, it appears to me that Emma implies talk accomplishes a lot, but it does so in the service of violence. When she claims "nothing got done," she is asserting that talk does not automatically oppose violence. Instead, lots of talking can appear to be inactive when, in actuality, it is extraordinarily active in ways that uphold the ongoing organization of violence. A slightly revised version of Emma's statement could more explicitly highlight the uneven actions of discourse: "There was lots of talking . . . And then nothing got done *to challenge the violent status quo.*" Without this clarification, talk that allows violence to continue could be mistaken as taking no action—as anything but muscular—and it could therefore remain an unintelligible aspect of the violence–organization relationship.

Some organizational scholars have made arguments similar to the one Emma makes. In the early years of human relations, managers would listen to employees during interviews. As many researchers have since pointed out, often employers had no intent—or even the authority—to make changes based on what they heard (Eisenberg & Witten, 1987; Hassard, 2012). In this management philosophy, listening deferred particular organizational actions (Tompkins & Wanca-Thibault, 2001), and many people have criticized Mayo and the human relations school for using listening to cultivate a complacent workforce whose needs were subordinated to those of management (e.g., Bruce & Nyland, 2011). Considered against the background of these arguments, PRU may be doing something quite right by insisting that its members cannot merely listen to complaints about sexual violence.

And yet, to assert that people at PRU cannot ignore sexual violence, PRU risks dismissing some forms of action that occur when people talk and listen to each other. Emma and others suggest that "rumors" and "chatter" accomplish nothing, and this claim helps to separate third-party reports (action against sexual violence) from "mere talk." This denigration of "rumors" and "chatter"—forms of gossip—may be extremely important. In the 19th century, groups of wealthy "gentlemen" used gossip to uphold their elite status, guard the boundaries of heterosexuality, and maintain their exclusive social ties (Milne-Smith, 2009). Per this historical reading, gossip can keep systems of power in place. Yet, because of their association with femininity, "rumors" and "chatter" are often devalued forms of speech (Spacks, 1982). Notes Meyers (2015), this kind of talk is used by people of all gender identities, yet

> it is generally dismissed as the mindless pastime of bored and malicious housewives or a pernicious form of social control carried out by catty teenage mean girls. [Its] bad reputation belies its importance as a space to make and circulate meaning outside of the dominant culture. . . . [It] prioritizes women's voices and concerns and allows gossipers to negotiate dominant culture together. (p. 71)

For Meyers, gossip does something and, more specifically, that "something" has to do with gendered inequality: Those without institutionalized power gossip to push back on and subvert the dominant culture. Others scholars have traced an affinity between gossip and queer politics, and they note that this form of talk can generate solidarity and manifest alternative intimacies (Cifor, 2016; Fackler, 2010; Holmes, 2015). Gossip often operates as an active form of talk that builds coalitions and resistance among people who do not have formal power in an organization. The notion of active gossip that Meyers and other scholars note does not square completely with Emma's comments about the "rumors" and "chatter" at Penn State. Emma points out that "rumors" and "chatter" did not stop Sandusky's violence, a point that usefully complicates the idea that talking about violence negates violence. Indeed, her statement may echo criticisms of gossip's historical use as a mechanism of oppression. Although Emma's comment thus intervenes in the persistent organization of violence, calling these forms of talk inactive also risks reinforcing the historical under-ascription of force to nondominant modes of talk. Active talk remains that which combats violence and thus, if talk does something, it is separate from violence. Inactive talk—the talk that allowed Sandusky's assaults to continue for years—simply does not do anything. Without a nuanced analysis of gendered/raced action and the power associated with it, the dismissal of rumors and chatter misses the uneven forces associated with talk. On the one hand, and as the authors I have mentioned help to point out, talk's supposed inactivity is an outcome of its association with women, feminized men, men and women of color, and people who are queer and/or gender nonbinary. But on the other hand, talk's so-called inactivity masks its active participation in the organization of violence.

PRU's insistence that listening be coupled with reporting exists in tension with what researchers know about how listening transforms trauma. In feminist and trauma studies, listening to accounts of violence is regarded as an agentic moment in and of itself (see Caruth, 2014). In their work on organizational trauma, Hope and Eriksen (2009) discussed agentic witnessing, which is "encouraging the facilitation of voice-claiming and experience-naming, without imposing one's own personal analysis" (p. 110). They suggested that those who have experienced sexual violence need to be in the presence of empathic listeners. They went on to argue that people who experience violence become agentic simply by speaking about the assault. For Hope and Eriksen, this kind of agency is crucial in organizational responses to violence because it avoids what many call "secondary victimization" (R. Campbell & Raja, 1999), wherein the organization makes decisions on behalf of the person who was assaulted. Often, the person who was assaulted lacks control and decisional power over how institutions respond, and that loss of control mimics the experience of the original assault. Responses other than mere listening, in this rationale, further disempower the person who has already been victimized. A community of trauma specialists concurs that compassionate listening transforms trauma (Birrell & Freyd, 2006; Herman, 1997). At PRU, the trouble seems to be sifting the transformational potential of listening from the kind of listening that seems to do very little because it upholds the standard, usual, (and violent) state of affairs.

Gendered/raced power dynamics influence whether listening is said to accomplish anything, and these dynamics—whereby discourse is imbued with uneven force—often benefit the organization. In one of my interviews with Title IX investigators, they mentioned that when complaints do not end with disciplinary action, investigators often have what they call "educational conversations" with the "respondent," the person whom the complaint was filed against. The enforcers and investigators argued that these interactions transform a culture of violence. They suggested that talking with someone about his problematic behavior and its consequences makes sexual violence less acceptable at PRU. In contrast to the argument that listening to complaints about sexual violence without subsequent reporting does not *do* anything, this argument suggests that a respondent who listens to enforcers of mandatory reporting changes. The things enforcers say to that respondent have an impact, and

their statements accomplish something. One key difference between the "educational conversations" and a rumor mill about
perpetrators is that the investigators have access to formal role
power at PRU while those people who "chatter" about their
experiences of assault do not. Tellingly, undergraduate student
activists charge investigators' "educational conversations" with
the same critique investigators level at those people who listen
to sexual violence disclosures without reporting: They say the
educational conversations do not do anything. That critique,
again, appears to reinforce the separation of talk from action.
With an analysis of power, though, a pattern starts to emerge
at PRU: Those kinds of talk associated with formalized organizational processes, roles, and procedures are considered active,
and those kinds of talk associated with marginalized groups
and perspectives are considered inactive. To the extent that the
organization's actions support marginalized groups—that is,
organizing processes dislodge sedimented inequities on the basis
of difference—the association between "active" talk and organization is useful. But if talk is "active" only when it reinforces the
organization, the assignment of activity can also serve to maintain persistent injustices.

With this idea in mind, the gendered and raced implications of
supposedly (in)active talk become more apparent. PRU excludes
some kinds of talk from the reporting processes: ones that could
challenge the organization's ongoing commitment to whiteness.
Enforcers of mandated reporting say that reportable instances of
violence, discrimination, and harassment must include names of
specific perpetrators. One of the enforcers said this:

> If someone is going so far as to *name* somebody else as causing
> them to feel uncomfortable or subjecting them to sexual
> harassment or . . . sexual assault, that is akin to making a
> specific complaint, that in my mind needs to be addressed

institutionally. Which is very different than just a dialogue around the issues . . . If they're going so far as to talk to a faculty member, to talk to a [mandated reporter], you know, that so-and-so has harassed me, has discriminated against me, has assaulted me, that is akin to raising a complaint to the institution that we have an obligation to address.

This enforcer distinguished dialogue (which does not require a report) and complaint (which requires a report) based on what people say about their own experiences of sexual violence. If a speaker does not name a perpetrator, the comments do not prompt mandated reports. If a speaker names a perpetrator, the comments must be reported.

This distinction allows those who have experienced violence to have some power to make decisions about whether those incidents get reported. But the boundaries the organization has created around what kind of speech is linked to subsequent organizational actions can legitimate nonresponsiveness even when an organizational member explicitly requests university action. Under the practices at PRU, if a university member says to a mandated reporter, "J. Smith committed violence against me on this campus, and I do not want the university to take any action," that statement must be reported. If, however, that university member says to a mandated reporter, "I have experienced violence on this campus and I want the university to do something about it," that statement does not have to be reported, and requires no formal university response. At the opening of this section, I highlighted the rationale that if people speak about violence, PRU assumes they do so because they want the assaults to stop (and, implicitly, the speaker wants the listener to report the incident). Yet this distinction between dialogue and complaint adds a layer of nuance to that rationale. PRU members may explicitly state their desire for organizational action, but the organization need not respond. Mere disclosure of experiences of sexual violence does not prompt formal organizational action. Instead, it is the presence or absence of a human's name that determines whether a listener must make a report. In this instance, the supposed action of discourse is linked directly to who/what is considered human.

As a consequence of these perimeters around active speech, the university can overlook some forms of violence. In the last chapter, I described the racial and gender justice forums in which students made repeated statements about their experiences of systemic oppression at the university. Because protestors and advocates did not name individuals in their testimonies, their speech was considered to be mere dialogue, the kind of speech that does not prompt reports or investigations. The requirement that those who experience sexual violence name a perpetrator means that any organized violence (i.e., violence endemic to broader organizational systems) does not get addressed through PRU's Title IX processes. I develop this argument in the next section of this chapter where I show that at PRU, the boundaries around "human," in connection to violence, reinforce the whiteness of the organization.

Talk and text at PRU are not uniformly attributed with agency. Instead, only some kinds of talk are considered to be active, and this "activity" is patterned by gender and race. Some talk is called inactive if it challenges persistent organizational power dynamics, as in the testimony about structural racism and related injustices from protestors. Other talk is called inactive if it actively supports the ongoing organization of violence, as in PRU members' descriptions of talk at Penn State. This analysis suggests that, contrary to some scholars' claims, discourse has not become too forceful, in general. Instead, the force of discourse depends upon complex gendered/raced processes through which violence materializes. As I detail in the next section, the processes that materialize violence also depend upon the relationship between "human" and "agent."

Dispersed agents can act, but only discrete (human) agents can commit sexual violence: The persistence of organized whiteness

Multiple gendered/raced boundary-making practices at PRU consolidate violence in discrete agents, and the requirement that members name perpetrators is only one example. Across many sites at PRU, individuals alone are said to commit violence. As a consequence, the systemic violence that many marginalized PRU members experience is less intelligible. Although nonhumans are repeatedly granted some capacity to act at PRU—sometimes in ways so powerful that they compel human action—those nonhumans are never granted a capacity for violent action. Because the agency necessary to commit violence is routinely located in a human entity, it becomes difficult to understand that organizational processes/actions materialize gendered/raced violence.

The attribution of violence to individuals occurs, for instance, in one of PRU's policies on violence. The word "individual" appears seven times and the word "persons" appears twice. Together, these two terms are the third most frequently used (after "police" and "behavior"). The policy specifies that "individuals" who are violent will be penalized. An alternative policy could state that "violent acts" will be penalized. The language implies that if collectives or nonhumans commit violent acts, those acts will go unpunished. In other words, the university explicitly states that it responds to humans who commit violence, and the possibility of other entities committing violence gets set aside in this policy language.

The explicit framing of violence as an individual act occurs elsewhere, too, and in some of these other places the racial implications of this framing are more apparent. For example, in a training session for graduate scholar–teachers, someone in the 400-person audience suggested that the examples of reportable incidents all seemed to be one-on-one. The audience member asked what would happen if a community targeted a person and lots of smaller events added up to a larger problem with violence. Following some discussion, the trainer said the offices that handle mandated reports would have a difficult time investigating and responding to that kind of complaint. She affirmed that mandated reporting—and the accompanying Title IX apparatus—responds to individuals' behavior. The trainer then went on to suggest that the phenomenon the questioner was asking about was best handled by the university's multicultural center because it was an issue of climate change, not violence. The trainer's categorization echoes the requirement that a reportable statement include a named perpetrator: To be considered violence, an incident must be tethered to a discrete agent. This exchange is a symptom of the racialized relationship between organization and violence at PRU.

The trainer effectively separates systemic, repeated, patterned harm from the category violence. Indeed, she states that these problems are *not* violence but culture. This boundary-making practice aligns Title IX processes with organized whiteness. The trainer says that when wrongdoing cannot clearly be attached to one individual, the office whose mission is to advocate for people of color and underrepresented students is supposed to address those issues. The trainer relegates responsibility for responding to many systemic oppressions—whether on the basis of race, gender, or sexuality—to the group on campus designated to address systemic racism. This move absolves PRU's Title IX offices from responding to most patterns of discrimination that cannot be encapsulated in one-on-one incidents. To separate patterns of discrimination and harassment from violence minimizes the severity of racism while also separating systemic racism from sexual violence. If systemic racism is not linked with sexual violence, then, by implication, the sexual violence that PRU's Title IX processes address is only that which is intelligible within the frame of whiteness. In many exchanges like this one, raced boundary-making practices around violence include the consolidation of agencies in a single human.

Though this consolidation of agencies in a human occurs repeatedly during discussions of (sexual) violence, agency is not uniformly the purchase of humans. Sometimes, nonhumans are assigned quite a bit of agency, but not during discussions about enacting violence. These nonhuman, dispersed agencies are noticeable, for instance, in conversations about ownership and authorship of the policies that establish the mandatory obligation to report. Ashley, a PRU official responsible for the school's sexual violence response processes, reviewed the informed consent sheet I had created for the study. She made this comment in response to a sentence that attributed ownership of a sexual violence policy to her office:

> Ashley: On the second page [of the consent form] you talk about, "If you're aware of the [Office of Violence Response's] policy." You know, one of the things that we try to remind people of is that the policy is not ours, it's the university's. We're the office that enforces it. So I would say, you know ... it gets a little bit complicated actually . . . . [One] policy was signed off by our chancellor. The other one is signed off by our president. So, you know, it's accurate to refer to them as the [PRU] policy.

Ashley challenges my attribution of policy ownership by naming multiple agents, none of which enforce and provide university-wide education on those policies. Throughout, Ashley affirms the university as an actor. She references two human agents, the chancellor and the president of the university, but rather than attribute authorship to those individuals, Ashley emphasizes the organization's responsibility for enacting and authoring the policy. Ashley allows that her office enforces the policy, but resists my suggestion that her office created or owned that policy. She advances an understanding of the organization that incorporates complex connections—and distributed agency—among policies, university leaders, and entities like Ashley's office or the president. Ashley's comments resonate with a feminist new materialist, non-entitative approach to agency. Yet her articulation of these complex and varied agencies contrasts with other discussions about the agency or agencies required to commit violence. Though some organizational actions—policy authorship, in this case—are diffuse, the locus of violence is consistently and repeatedly attached exclusively to an individual human.

This difference between discrete human agency and diffuse organizational agencies sets up uneven power dynamics. In some instances, PRU members suggest that nonhuman agencies are so strong and powerful that they command human action. This idea shows up in an interview I conducted with Sarah, who, because of her role as a PRU mental health counselor, is exempt from mandated reporting. When I asked her to describe the advice she offers to those who need to make mandated reports, her answer led me to understand that multiple ideas about agency occur in the discourse on mandated reporting, but that some of those ideas are prioritized. Sarah said this:

> We all can make choices. We can all break the law and walk across the street without—you know, when it says not

to walk, and I do that the same. . . . I let them [mandated reporters who seek my advice] know what the policy is and that that's what the university expects of them, but it's still their—I don't like to say that because . . . someone from [one of the enforcement offices] [would say], "It's not their choice! They don't have a choice. That's the policy."

Sarah's initial acknowledgment that policies cannot compel people to action is of particular importance. In contrast to her first statement, she points to an interpretation of agency that she attributes to one of the offices that enforces mandated reporting. In that second interpretation, the policy's agency eclipses the agency of the mandated reporter. Sarah interrupts the phrase, "it's still their choice." Before uttering the word "choice," Sarah acknowledges that she does not like to indicate that mandated reporters can decide whether to comply with the policy. She suggests that her hesitation occurs because those who enforce the policy would claim otherwise. Sarah's efforts to mark these different positions in the discourse around mandated reporting, and her reluctance to suggest that mandated reporters have decisional capacity, evidences the uneven ways in which words, texts, and humans are attributed with the power to act. Importantly, she implies that it is in the organization's interests to maintain that organizational documents—authored through processes that involve multiple entities—are more powerful than individual humans who make conscious decisions about their own actions.

Although some nonhuman agencies are intelligible at PRU, they are not universally powerful. As the last two examples suggest, even as the university affirms its own capacity to act, it simultaneously denies that capacity to other collective agencies and some individual agents. Although Ashley mentioned two individual humans, she did so to assert that the policy was not attributable to any human actor. She affirmed the organization's capacity to act through dispersed agents. Sarah's comments highlighted that the intelligibility of this collective actor—the organization—is prioritized. She was reluctant to acknowledge individual human choice because some university offices framed and discussed their reporting policies as more powerful than human decisions. The simultaneous affirmation of the organization as an actor and the denial of individual agency resonates with the claims of organizational scholars who noted that policies often "reduce the human actor to an intermediary, thereby reaffirming the existence of the organization" (Cooren, 2004, p. 379). Both Ashley's and Sarah's comments cast human actors as go-betweens that infuse the organization with a capacity to act. At times at PRU, individual human agency is eclipsed by the larger organization.

Although PRU readily accepts that nonhumans and dispersed nonentities are powerful actors, this understanding of action and agencies does not apply to violence. In discussions of rape and other forms of sexual violence, the human actor is never an "intermediary" who acts at the behest of organizational policies and processes. Instead, that human is a full, discrete agent. The university seems to benefit from this contrast. PRU maintains that its own forms of agency are forceful enough to stop and/or respond to violence, but its agencies are not so powerful that they are complicit in enacting violence. These boundary-making practices keep the university focused only *on* the rapist, not beyond the rapist.

It's hardly surprising that PRU insists that individual humans commit violence. Liberalism is a key tenet of many organizations in the United States, and Title IX, the Clery Act, and the Violence Against Women Act are all part of this cultural and legal framework. Yet this focus on individuals as the sole agents of violence becomes troubling when we consider how the ascription of violent force to humans, but not larger entities, links with whiteness. C. I. Harris (1993) said, "The law has recognized and codified racial group identity as an instrumentality of exclusion and exploitation; however, it has refused to recognize group identity when asserted by racially oppressed groups as a basis for affirming or claiming rights" (p. 1761). These moves—acknowledging dispersed agencies in the service of exclusion but refusing dispersed agency when asserted by oppressed groups—happen at PRU. The trainer at the educational session for graduate scholar–teachers suggested that if a community targets and violates a member of a marginalized group, that pattern is not violence and the university's multicultural center should respond. Similarly, in response to marginalized students' statements about ongoing violence and discrimination, PRU insists that, absent of named perpetrators, these statements are dialogue and therefore operate outside its Title IX processes. The selective acknowledgment and denial of dispersed action aligns PRU's Title IX processes with whiteness.

Contrary to the critique that discourse has become too powerful or too active, at PRU, the actions of discourse are narrowly conscribed, and they are interconnected with the boundary-making practices around the (non)human. The requirement for a named perpetrator maintains that statements are active (a) only when they represent violence, and (b) only when an individual human committed the represented violence. By implication, discourse remains outside the realm of violence, as do the impacts of dispersed agents. In this context, I am reluctant to support theorizing that cedes discourse as any less forceful without attention to power and the processes by which "human" action coalesces. To do so would reinforce the mechanisms by which violence gets organized in relationship to difference.

Making the violence–organization relationship intelligible: Interrogating access to "human" and "agency"

In his critique of constitutive approaches, Reed (2005) suggested that social construction leaves the field of organization studies "'ontologically mute' because it claims that the realities that we deal with are essentially a product of everyday language" (p. 1624). Reed uses an ableist metaphor in this argument, and noticing it is important. He complains that the real is left without agency, that it cannot *do* anything because discourse does everything. Reed arrives at this claim by suggesting that reality cannot speak. Speaking and doing seem folded up in one another and, indeed, an ability to act and an ability to speak seem nearly indistinguishable in his argument. Even when he argues against the oversubscription of agency to discourse, Reed still relies on the rationale he critiques: Action, a capacity to impact the world, is measured through a metaphorical ability to wield language. An uncareful coupling of agency and speech is hardly unique to Reed: Feminist new materialists also substitute one for the other as if they are equivalents. For example, Geertz and van der Tuin (2013) argued that feminist new materialism refuses the common bisection of "representations being active and the represented being mute" (p. 175). Rather than suggest that representations are active and the represented are inactive, these authors suggest that the represented cannot talk. Even in scholarship that pays careful attention to difference, "active" and "able to speak" appear to be synonymous.

Acknowledging and problematizing this speech–agency conflation is particularly important for theorizing violence because both speech and agency have served as proxies for the designation "human." When organizations claim that some discourse is inactive and nonagentic, they effectively limit the agency of speech. Scholars who assert discourse has become overly agentic might be sympathetic to this claim. Yet the separation of speech and agency also splits discourse from violence. After all, surely the inert and the inactive—as the feminine has so often been described—cannot commit violence. This limitation around the action of discourse sets the boundary practices around human into motion: If speech and agency are decoupled, passive (or nonagentic) people—as women have often been stereotyped—may now be fully human. The category begins to seem a bit less exclusive. And perhaps those people of color—women, men, and nonbinary individuals—who through racist stereotypes have been repeatedly characterized as actively violent yet inarticulate also must be admitted. Conveniently, the limits on the action of discourse make "human" more all-encompassing and also push violence outside the category's bounds. The coupled expansion and contraction of "human" preserves the whiteness and masculinity of its prerequisites.

For these reasons, I meet organizational scholarship's material turn with some suspicion. As the fragile exclusions that maintain "human" threaten to democratize access to the category, the field of organizational research has made a dramatic shift. Scholars have become interested in matter again—and its activity—just at the social/political/intellectual moment when "human" has become more capacious. Discourse—that supposedly feminized, inactive phenomenon—has acquired some muscle, and mainstream folks definitely do not like butch women. The complaint that discourse is on steroids, that it has become too muscular, and that it does too much seems to be a retrenchment of the gendered and racialized order. I hear the critique as a complaint that femininity appears in drag and whiteness has lost its potency. The charge seems really to be that soft communication—which has served white supremacy—has become tough, angular, able to wield force. I am sympathetic to many aspects of a material turn, and I see significant political potential in a less anthropocentric understanding of agency. Even as organizational communication scholars make these intellectual shifts, they should not lose sight of the ways in which these shifts can both buttress and undo patriarchy and white supremacy. Critical scholars, in particular, have good reason to amplify the muscularity of discourse even as many of them work to problematize the (non)human.

5

Beyond the rapist

Rethinking communication and agency, changing campus rape

As the book has progressed, I have advanced two central claims. First, I argued that violence communicates in ways that defy simple representation. Using a feminist new materialist lens that posits violence as intra-active, several common refrains about violence (e.g., speech opposes violence, reports merely describe assaults) are no longer tenable. To refuse the material-discourse divide requires different claims: Language does not stand apart from violence, and counting assaults is not a simple endeavor. When rape is conceptualized in this way, denying evidence of sexual violence is challenging. Second, I argued that understandings of "human" and "agency" shape the relationship between organization and sexual violence. Feminist new materialism asserts that agency and the (non)human are intertwined. I used that idea—in conversation with arguments from critical race scholars—to show that organizations depend on the uneven force of discourse to intervene in some violent processes while maintaining others. In this chapter, to give a sense for how these arguments transfer beyond PRU, I summarize these claims and illustrate their applicability in other contexts.

Violence communicates differently: Insisting on pure representation stalls transformation

Despite the utility of descriptions that correspond to sexual violence, organizing around them has serious limitations. As I argued in Chapter 3, the logic of representation is embedded in the systems of inequity upon which violence is predicated. The very idea that communication simply represents the world carries with it assumptions about and implications for race, gender, and sexuality. In earlier chapters, I provided several examples in which PRU insisted that accurate assault counts—or direct representation of a named perpetrator—must precede any action from the school. This rationale allowed PRU to defer addressing sexual violence in meaningful ways, even while it intervened in some problematic forms of inaction. The idea that representation is purely discursive, and the deployment of that idea to delay other forms of action, is hardly unique to PRU. Indeed, many groups explicitly committed to combatting sexual violence use the same rationale.

The idea appeared, for example, in past federal efforts to curb U.S. campus rape. Under the Obama administration, the government directed more resources toward sexual violence prevention and response. Notalone.gov, the hub for information associated with these efforts, encouraged campuses to conduct climate surveys. These tools can be an important supplement to reporting data, which are consistently low. Even so, the website's rationale for surveys held representation apart from the world. The website said, "Campus climate surveys are essential because they generate data on the nature and extent of sexual assault on campuses, as well as campus attitudes surrounding sexual assault. Armed with accurate data, administrators and students can then begin to direct resources where they are most needed" (Office on Violence Against Women, 2017, para. 10). The word "then" in the second sentence marks a distinction between collecting information—generating accurate representations—and directing resources that fuel sustained change. Having multiple kinds of knowledge—official reports *and* surveys, for example—is useful and important, but the split between creating representations and taking action is objectionable. The survey is itself a form of action, one that, when continually cited as a precursor for other actions, ends up slowing or halting change. The website's use of the word "armed" underscores this point. Representations, in this passage, are cast as symbolic weapons that combat violence. Because the passage positions "data" in this way, readers might easily assume a widely accepted but problematic idea: Discourse is only used to counter violence. By contrast, insisting on a particular kind of data—the representations notalone.gov advocates—can actually buttress violence.

This emphasis on simple representations and counts is especially problematic because it creates space for fiction. In a separate FAQ document from the same source, the response to "Why are campus climate surveys important?" read, "Decades of research has shown that victims rarely report sexual assault to law enforcement, and in many cases do not even access formal services, such as crisis centers. The result is that official statistics may not represent the full extent of the problem on any one campus" (Office on Violence Against Women, 2016, para. 3). The phrase "may not" in this excerpt implies some uncertainty about whether "official statistics" are accurate reflections of reality. The passage could say "official statistics *do not* represent the full extent of the problem" or "official statistics *rarely, if ever,* represent the full extent of the problem." Either alternative wording would sustain clarity around the facts in the first sentence of the passage. Instead, the site's use of "may not" implies that campuses—and the federal government—are not sure whether "official" counts match sexual assault rates. Furthermore, the passage insinuates that, though "official statistics may not" be fully representative, information that *is* fully representative is still achievable. It positions that more complete data at some point in the future. By this rationale, one major focus for assault "prevention" should be creating accurate, representative counts. The problem, of course, is that this knowledge already exists. It is already here and now, not something to arrive at a later date. Researchers, educators, and activists already have plenty of expertise about the prevalence and incidence of sexual assault, and that expertise is more than enough to drive thoughtful, informed, and effective changes on campuses.

When fully accurate representations are understood as an inevitable, eventual achievement, multiple consequences follow. First, organizations can stall: It would seem unwise to act and make changes if a campus does not yet know how often rape is happening. This argument overlooks not only that knowledge about prevalence is available but also that waiting for fully representative counts is, in itself, a form of action. Organizations and their members can also invent tales that not only are completely disconnected from what is already known but also derail efforts to address public health and move toward justice. As I was revising this book, U.S. Secretary of Education Betsy DeVos made a series of public statements and decisions advancing the idea that, under Title IX, countless innocent students are wrongfully accused of rape and, subsequently, their lives are ruined. Her arguments were neither new nor unique, but DeVos made them from a position of extraordinary power and influence. She was flat-out wrong that an epidemic of false accusations exists; it does not (Lonsway, Archambault, & Lisak, 2009). False reports of car theft happen at about the same rate as those of rape, but it is hard to imagine someone suggesting that the small number of false reports of stolen cars provides a good reason to dismantle the system of investigation that brings thieves to justice. If we did not know how often cars were stolen or how often thefts were falsely reported, then we would turn our energy to figuring those numbers out, and it might make sense to stop all action for quite some time. After all, maybe 90% of reported car thefts happen when a vindictive person wants to trash the reputation of his neighbor, get some attention, and maybe make a little money from insurance. This argument surrounds campus rape. If it seems like universities do not know how often rape actually happens, how could they possibly assess the accuracy of claims about it? The idea that representation is the best way to know about rape—and that accurate counts will arrive someday—helps organizations to address neither the already well-established high incidence of sexual assault nor its deleterious impacts on community and individual health.

Organizations need to reframe the evidence they deem persuasive. Instead of waiting for a particular kind of representation, organizations would do better to adopt a tenet of feminist new materialism: 100% accurate representations will never be available. Frost (2011) said that feminist new materialism requires "an acknowledgement of the impossibility of full and definitive knowledge and a corollary surrender of the teleological assumption that we might possibly, at some future point, achieve [it]" (p. 79). Framing knowledge in this way means that organizations cannot wait to change. Instead, they must take action based upon myriad knowledges that already provide a clear and accurate, but never complete, account of the violence that occurs.

Agency organizes violence: A sole focus on individual humans obscures power

My second central contention is that scholars who theorize the violence–organization relationship should consider the connections between agency and the (non)human. If speech is associated with being human, and if being human is a precondition for having agency, then that which cannot speak is not only inhuman but also does not have agency. Moreover, if violence is unable to speak—if it is separate from communication—it is outside the realm of humanity. Although distancing violence from humanity could be useful for those who want to condemn violence, that distance also creates terrible twin consequences. When violence is considered inhuman, people cannot always acknowledge their own violence. And when people and organizations do acknowledge human violence, they often do so when the perpetrators are members of groups that the dominant population would like to see as less than fully human. That dehumanization legitimates ongoing violence.

To complicate matters further, to be an agent often requires a capacity for committing violence. Those who cannot commit violence in any given moment—for example, those people who experience violence—seem un-agentic and in need of rescue. These targets of violence are cast as victims, not agents. When agency is the antithesis to victimization, several paradoxes result: A person who commits or experiences violence seems less human, but in order to be a fully agentic human, one must be able to commit violence, even if one does not actually enact it. These complexities are sometimes resolved through pervasive victim-blaming. If people who experience violence are agentic— that is, responsible for the crime—then the person who commits violence against them is not actually violent, thus still human.

At the same time, the people who "invite" crime upon themselves seem to willingly eliminate their own agency. Society can then argue that those who experience violence do not want to be human because they do not want to be agents. These complex rhetorical moves preserve the status of those who commit sexual violence, people who are far more likely than not to be members of dominant groups.

Current debates about gun ownership in the United States further illustrate some of these paradoxes around the concepts human, agency, and violence. The ubiquitous threat of an "armed gunman" on campuses and in K–12 schools conjures images, for many, of helpless students and teachers who need to be saved. They are potential victims of violence. In this moment, their vulnerability—which is often equated with lack of agency—may make them seem less than fully human. Many advocates for concealed carry on campuses argue that a person with a hidden weapon can disarm the attacker. That person is assumed to be good and right and is not ever framed as a potential threat. Instead, the person with a hidden weapon is cast as a savior, one who defends. This concealed carrier has the perpetual capacity for violence and, by having a gun on his body, makes that threat continually present. Those who advocate for concealed carry maintain a delicate balance: The concealed carrier is always able to enact violence but never actually does so. He has enough capacity for violence to be a fully agentic human, and he offers others protection against being victimized, an experience that would diminish their full agency. He restores the teachers/students to the category "human."

The humanness of the man with the concealed weapon is buoyed through contrast to the "armed gunman" who, by shooting indiscriminately, is cast as less than human. The armed gunman trope is continuously associated with mental illness: Numerous public accounts describe "active shooters" as crazy, deranged, unhinged. Given this monster as a foil, the person with the concealed weapon has a justifiable target. If the concealed carrier fires at the armed gunman, the concealed carrier becomes neither an active shooter nor an armed gunman, even though both these descriptions are technically accurate. The difference has to do with the complex ways in which violence, and its links to agency, patterns who is valuable. This logic around concealed carry, which is hardly ever explicit, is employed to relax regulations on gun ownership. In turn, this relaxation expands the pool of people—mostly white men—who can threaten or enact violence without dominant social groups categorizing it as such.

People may, at times, need to use violence to defend themselves from violence, but public discussions of self-defense are often limited by unidirectional, individual understandings of power: One human initiated, the other human responded. Stripped of broader context, people pay attention only to the immediate moment. When public discussions of violence are patterned by this myopia, society cannot think in more rigorous ways about how individual humans who enact violence are continually embedded in histories prior to themselves and, most importantly, how those histories implicate multifaceted power dynamics.

As a result, people often overlook violence committed by those with the most power and ignore the double-binds that simultaneously admit and exclude nondominant people to and from the category "human." Under the current logic, those individuals who are not part of the most powerful groups must prove their ability to commit violence in order to be human. Paradoxically, if they enact violence, the reason for their exclusion from the category "human" is confirmed. The invisibility of some violence occurs in the following hypothetical example of a married, opposite-sex, cisgendered couple who is experiencing conflict.

The woman points a gun at the man and threatens to shoot him. To protect himself, the man shoots her first. He was certain his life was in danger. Without looking further, many people would judge that the man rightfully defended himself. This evaluation, though, misses other facts: The man had been abusing his wife for the last 10 years, had previously threatened to shoot and kill her, and had raped her multiple times. Without attention to the couple's history, it is not possible to consider that the woman was defending herself against the man's pattern of ongoing violence and abuse. Instead, the violence she was experiencing goes unnoticed.

Though expanding the time frame around the couple gives a more comprehensive understanding of the situation, it still overlooks a broader societal context that hides elements of violence. Marital rape was not a crime in all 50 U.S. states until 1993. Prior to then, when women said "I do" at the altar, they entered a legal agreement that gave their husbands unfettered access to their bodies at any time, regardless of their in-the-moment consent to sexual activity. For many years, marriage was a system of ownership in which women were the legal property of their husbands. If the focus is only the immediate moment, or even only the history of the couple, those who apply or deny the label "violence" can have amnesia about the continuing legacy of these histories in the present. When violence is radically contextualized with an historical analysis sensitive to power dynamics, it becomes far more difficult to see violence only in the woman's raised gun. Instead, we have to think beyond the immediate moment when assessing the agencies of violence.

Because of the paradoxical associations I have outlined, when scholars rethink agency, they must keep questions about difference at the fore. A simple move toward a more capacious, posthuman understanding of agency is problematic because it ignores the uneven capacities granted to discourse as well as uneven access to the category "human." Without thoughtfulness, scholars can use posthumanism to preserve inequities based on gender, race, and sexuality that are part of the system of violence. On the other hand, not to rethink agency is also problematic: Current iterations of the concept retain a focus on individual, isolated, violent events that make violence seem ahistorical and acontextual.

Moving beyond the rapist: Other cases and contexts

I have hinted at how my analysis of organizational sexual violence transfers to other contexts. To show this transferability in more detail, I discuss two additional cases. The first case extends my arguments to the legal standards used to assess whether a U.S. school responded appropriately to campus sexual violence. The second case shows how the analysis in this book can offer insights about sexual violence in a different organizational context: women's gymnastics organizations in the United States.

Case 1: Reconsidering actual notice and deliberate indifference

In the broad legal apparatus that shapes university responses to Title IX, I see a struggle over how to conceptualize agency and the discourse–materiality relationship. When courts err toward individualized agency and a discourse–materiality split, decisions tend to favor the status quo and undermine justice for survivors. This struggle, and some of these negative consequences, are evident in discussions of the legal standards that determine whether a school is responsible for sexual violence.

In private lawsuits, to be found liable for poor or improper responses to sexual violence, a school must have "actual notice" of the violence, and the school must display "deliberate indifference" in its response to that knowledge. Actual notice occurs when a school official who has the capacity and authority to address sexual violence is made aware of an incident. Deliberate indifference is "an intentional failure to act in a situation where remedial action is required" (Sokolow, n.d., p. 1). Both of these standards were developed in a number of cases, notably *Gebser v. Lago Vista Independent School District* and *Davis v. Monroe County Board of Education*.

Some courts have interpreted actual notice, which is sometimes called actual knowledge, to include a narrow set of representations of violence. Usually, courts consider reports that (a) identify individual perpetrators and (b) are delivered to designated campus officials to be actual notice. Similar to my argument about PRU's reporting practices, actual notice also relies upon a separation between discourse and materiality. This split is evident in *A.W. v. Humble Independent School District*. In that case, the mother of an underage high school student told the school about her daughter's "improper relationship" with a teacher, but the school took no action. After graduation, when the student said she had been "sexually molested," then the school took action. The judge found that, because the student's mother had told the school about an improper relationship, but had not explicitly indicated that the relationship was sexual, the school did not have actual notice.

The judge made this argument despite these facts: (a) multiple students and parents complained about the relationship between the student and teacher; (b) school officials said they would investigate these complaints but did not; (c) school officials saw the student and teacher leave the school alone, almost daily, for approximately two years; (d) school officials noted that the student and teacher were spending inordinate amounts of time together, often alone in the teacher's office; (e) school officials also noted that the student's grades dropped dramatically and that the student withdrew from peers; and (f) school officials knew that the student and teacher shared a bed while on school-related, out-of-town trips. The judge emphasized that school officials never directly observed any sexual conduct. This argument allows schools to ignore myriad signs of abusive relationships, many of which were present in this case. The judge interpreted actual notice such that either specific words about sexual assault had to be uttered or school officials had to observe a physical sexual assault. This requirement rests on the notion that violence is solely physical and, moreover, that verbal indicators of violence must directly represent a physical assault.

Assumptions about individual agency also shape both actual notice and deliberate indifference. In some interpretations of actual notice, schools must be made aware of individual perpetrators. In one case, however, *Simpson v. University of Colorado*, a court found that the school had actual notice of a generalized risk of assault resulting from the university's own policies (K. L. Harris, 2013). This reasoning pushes past an understanding of individualized, violent agency. More often, cases rely exclusively on individualized agency in assessing both actual notice and deliberate indifference. For example, as described in *Patterson v. Hudson Area Schools*, a young gay man was repeatedly subjected to bullying, taunting, and harassment based on his sexual identity. The middle school he attended took some action, including putting him in a different class. Though the original perpetrators stopped their problematic behavior, over several years, other students began harassing the boy. These incidents escalated, despite repeated requests from the boy's family that the school district take action. Eventually, a new and different perpetrator sexually assaulted the boy in the school's locker room. The district court found, however, that the school was not deliberately indifferent because they had taken action based on notice about known perpetrators. The court suggested that the school's failure to stop the violence or harassment from other individuals was irrelevant. In this instance, both legal standards focused on individual perpetrators of violence to the neglect of a more generalized risk of violence against a person. Notably, that person was a member of a marginalized group that experiences extremely high rates of sexual violence. Eventually, the Sixth Circuit overturned this ruling and suggested that the school was responsible not for any one incident of harassment by an individual perpetrator, but for an ongoing pattern of harassment.

In the original case, Hudson Area Schools argued that they could not be held responsible for stopping *new* perpetrators. This interpretation of deliberate indifference implies that schools would be responsible for stopping known, repeat perpetrators. However, in some cases, even when an individual perpetrator assaulted multiple people, courts have emphasized that the school is still not responsible if it had no notice of assaults against the specific victim. So, for example, in *Wills v. Brown University*, a student reported to the school that a professor had sexually assaulted her while she was in his office. When the same thing happened a second time to a different student, a trial court found that the reports about the previous incident did not constitute actual notice, and thus the school was neither deliberately indifferent nor liable for the second incident. The school eventually took action after six more students had the same experience with the same professor.

I am hardly alone in criticizing these standards. Verna Williams, a law professor who argued one of the most important Title IX cases before the Supreme Court, is among others who have made similar observations. Speaking of a key case that established standards for actual notice and deliberate indifference, she said that "the Court laid a faulty foundation that erroneously construed sexual harassment as an individualized harm rather than a systemic form of discrimination" (Kuznick & Ryan, 2008, p. 391). Catharine MacKinnon, a widely recognized feminist legal scholar, made a similar claim that courts have misinterpreted deliberate indifference to deny that harassment is a group-based harm. She advocated that courts adopt the international human rights standard, due diligence, instead. Moreover, speaking of the requirement for actual notice, she argued that "should notice matter, one might think that schools are already, in advance, amply aware of the high risk of each incident of sexual harassment occurring, given the data on sexual harassment" (MacKinnon, 2016, p. 2089). These criticisms from legal experts resonate with mine, though the starting point for my argument is somewhat different. I am underscoring how unnamed ideas about the discourse–materiality relationship (*communication*) and about who or what can act (*agency*) operate in these decisions and the broader legal framework that shapes what happens at U.S. universities.

Case 2: A violent status quo at USA Gymnastics

As in discussions of the legal standard deliberate indifference, when organizations emphasize individual agency and representational accounts of violence, justice for survivors is delayed or nonexistent. In cases that involved USA Gymnastics, I see little debate over how to conceptualize agency and the discourse–materiality relationship. Instead, these concepts were uniformly deployed in ways that allowed perpetrators to continue assaulting while the organization resisted accountability.

USA Gymnastics oversees more than 3,000 member gyms across the United States. It also identifies and develops talented gymnasts who will compete at elite levels, including at the

Olympics. From 2014 through 2016, media outlets scrutinized the organization following a growing number of public complaints. Several gymnasts asserted that coaches and medical professionals had sexually assaulted them. In one high-visibility case in 2014, a recent graduate of Michigan State University said faculty member and medical doctor Larry Nassar had abused her. The school's police investigation found no violation of the university's policy. After that case, complaints and charges accumulated. An Olympic gymnast who competed in the early 2000s filed a lawsuit in California. She said Nassar had assaulted her between 1994 and 2000 while she was under his care. Another gymnast sued Nassar for assaulting her during 1996 and 1997 while she was a teenager. She said that while Nassar was treating her every six weeks for back pain, he would penetrate her vagina with his fingers for up to an hour per medical visit. This suit was filed on the same day as another three charges against Nassar for criminal sexual assault. Those other charges said Nassar assaulted a female victim in his home. When those assaults occurred between 1998 and 2005, the victim was less than 13 years old. By November 2016, Michigan State University police were investigating complaints from 50 different people who said Nassar abused or assaulted them. In December 2016, Nassar was arrested on federal child pornography charges. As of the end of 2016, 13 women and girls—mostly past and present gymnasts from Michigan—planned to sue Michigan State University regarding Nassar's misconduct. By late 2017, the number of plaintiffs in that case and eight other related cases— all nine of which were treated together in federal court—had grown to 140. In early 2018, the cases concluded when Nassar was sentenced to up to 175 years in prison.

Many people have suggested that, for years, Nassar was insulated from questions about his crimes. For much of his career, the gymnastics community celebrated and lauded him.

Nassar was the team doctor for the U.S. Olympic gymnastics team between 1996 and 2015, and he was awarded "United States Women's Gymnastics Elite Coaches Association National Contributor of the Year" six different times. The Olympic gymnast who filed the California lawsuit suggested that Bela and Marta Karolyi, revered coaches for elite and Olympic gymnasts, knew about Nassar's sexual assaults but did nothing.

To show why Nassar had not been caught or disciplined earlier, the *Indianapolis Star* published information about four different instances, none involving Nassar, in which USA Gymnastics had not alerted police to allegations of child abuse, sexual assault, or sexual misconduct. One case involved 2010 National Women's Coach of the Year, Marvin Sharp. In 2011, USA Gymnastics received a complaint about Sharp assaulting underage girls, but the organization did not report the information to the police. After USA Gymnastics received another allegation against Sharp in 2015, they did go to the police. Sharp was charged with child molestation and sexual misconduct in federal court, and he later committed suicide in jail. Another instance involved coach William McCabe. In 1998, USA Gymnastics received multiple complaints about him. In 1999, he began assaulting a girl but was not charged for those assaults until 2006, and he continued coaching in the interim. On the whole, the *Indianapolis Star*'s report suggested that USA Gymnastics protected coaches and failed to take action to stop assault against young female gymnasts.

The frameworks I have developed in this book call attention to several noteworthy aspects of these cases. First, media accounts attributed agency to multiple actors. Unlike many public discussions about sexual assault, the media did not suggest that the victimized girls had the capacity to stop the violence. Instead, the media scrutinized Nassar and coaches who were aware of the assaults. They also suggested that gym owners could have stopped the violence and that USA Gymnastics' policies were problematic. Though the media accounts distributed agency across multiple actors—policies, coaches, owners, other officials—they blamed two organizations for the brunt of wrongdoing: Michigan State University, where Nassar was an associate professor, and USA Gymnastics.

For the public to blame an organization for sexual assault—rather than individual perpetrators or victims—is somewhat unusual because it requires looking beyond the rapist. At PRU, the public rarely blamed the university but instead focused on individual perpetrators, victims, and units within the school. When sexual violence occurs at other universities, usually the organization is not the most frequently blamed entity. Publically blaming an organization is not altogether unheard of, however. In some of my previously published work, my co-author and I showed that when victims or perpetrators are implicated in a narrative about national identity, local organizations rather than individuals often take the blame (K. L. Harris & Hanchey, 2014). In the case of USA Gymnastics, several of the women who were assaulted were competing in international venues where gymnasts and other athletes were symbols of their home countries. To discount their stories—and suggest that the women were lying—would call into question the character of the United States, not simply the individual athletes. To blame the organization, however, does not interfere with the complex nationalistic meanings associated with the bodies of these young women. In early 2018, the persistence of a focus on the rapist—not beyond him—returned when the media again concentrated on Nassar and his sentencing, less so on the systems that supported him.

Very much like PRU, USA Gymnastics' own discussions of sexual violence focused almost wholly on individual perpetrators. The organization publishes a list of permanently banned, former members who coached gymnasts at all ages and levels. The overwhelming majority of people on the list are men. As of 2017, a full 89% of the reasons listed for a member being banned were related to sexual misconduct or abuse. A list like this is notably different from the information other organizations make available. For example, in the Catholic Church, members who commit sexual assault simply move from one site to the next without churchgoers having a way to know about that person's history. USA Gymnastics' list publication may be laudable in contrast to some other organizations, but it also problematically implies that expunging perpetrators is the primary key to ending sexual violence. Because the list demonstrates that the organization is eliminating members for misconduct, it may deflect blame and criticism from the organization. A focus on individuals can distract from questions about whether USA Gymnastics is eliminating problematic processes and systems: It may focus exclusively *on* rather than *beyond* the rapist.

Second, as in the case of PRU, the residue of representationalism, along with a discourse–materiality divide, gets used to resist organizational transformation and accountability. USA Gymnastics received written complaints from two different gym owners regarding coach William McCabe's misconduct. Both gym owners had terminated McCabe following inappropriate comments and behavior. USA Gymnastics, however, did not notify police of suspected child abuse because the complaints did not come directly from victims or their parents. Indeed, in legal testimony, USA Gymnastics acknowledged that it hardly ever forwarded complaints to the authorities. In one of the letters complaining about McCabe, gym owner Dan Dickey expressed frustration with this aspect of USA Gymnastics' policy. Dickey said that a USA Gymnastics officer had stated that "the law doesn't allow us to do anything without a formal complaint from a parent," and Dickey had no such complaint. USA Gymnastics' own statement on its website, on a page titled "How USA Gymnastics Combats Sexual Misconduct," says, "The duty to report lies with those who have first-hand knowledge . . . USA Gymnastics' grievance process requires that a formal complaint be filed by those directly involved, or if the aggrieved party is a minor, the parent may sign the complaint." This emphasis on first-hand knowledge undercuts an approach that focuses beyond the rapist. It overlooks that the majority of people who experience sexual assaults do not report them, even if they speak about them with community members. Under this logic, if community members saw multiple signs of abuse but the person experiencing that abuse was either unwilling or unable to make a formal complaint, the organization could rightfully do nothing. Not only does USA Gymnastics require a descriptive—thus representative—account of the incident, but it also combines that requirement with a narrow conception of agency: Only the person with direct experience, or that person's parent, can initiate a complaint. The idea runs counter to laws in many states across the United States that require individuals to report any instance of suspected child abuse to police, regardless of whether the abused or the abused person's parent makes a formal complaint or can provide a direct, representative description of the incidents.

USA Gymnastics' focus on individual agency is so extreme that in a legal briefing, its representatives argued that the organization was not responsible for reporting suspected child abuse to authorities. They argued that the reporting burden was attached only to individuals, not the organization. The prosecutor responded by noting that "there are individuals in any organization," so USA Gymnastics' argument would make it impossible for an organization ever to be responsible for reporting violence (Kwiatkowski & Evans, 2016, para. 46). In other arguments about the organization's reporting practices, Stephen Penny, the president of USA Gymnastics, explained some of the reasoning for not sending all complaints to the police. In a 2014 deposition, he said, "It's possible that someone may make a claim like this be-cause they don't like someone or because they heard a rumor or because they received information through other third parties." This logic is troubling: The organization does not report claims of suspected child abuse because they could be false, but it also has no process to determine whether a complaint is false. The only assessment is whether the complaint came directly from the abused minor or the parent of that minor.

USA Gymnastics' dismissal of rumors echoes my analysis of PRU in some ways. Both organizations require a representation of violence before investigating. At PRU, a statement about as-sault must include a named perpetrator. At USA Gymnastics, the requirement is more extreme: The direct description of as-sault must come from the affected party and cannot come from a third party, as it can at PRU. Both PRU and USA Gymnastics discount rumors, but at PRU, the system of mandated reporting is intended to ensure that well-known rumors are reported and investigated, even though that intention does not always play out in practice. USA Gymnastics insists on a narrower understanding of representative reports, and that understanding justifies the organization's lack of intervention when violence occurs. That lack of intervention is part of how violence is organized.

The insights I develop in this book also call attention to the gendered aspects of the sport, something that goes without men-tion in public and legal discussions of these cases. As part of the statement defending the policy of only responding to complaints filed directly by victims and victims' parents, the organization's president—Penny—cited the possibility for a "witch hunt" if un-substantiated claims were taken seriously. "Witch hunts" were used to persecute women who had violated the norms of femi-ninity without having committed any other wrongdoing. Penny's comparison does not work because the targeted wrongdoers are entirely members of the dominant gendered class. Furthermore, by committing violence, the suspected perpetrators are acting in accordance with the norms of hegemonic masculinity, not contrary to them. This problematic metaphor is used in the context of a sport in which young females are the overwhelming majority of participants, but adult males are in positions of power. According to USA Gymnastics, a full 85% of participants in the sport are female. The gender of coaches, however, does not reflect the high number of women in the sport. During the 2014–2015 school year, more than 47% of Division I women's gymnastics coaches were men. Focusing beyond the rapist requires keeping these gendered dynamics and power differences in view, not simply focusing on the presence or absence of individual assaults.

In both of these cases—that considering "deliberate indifference" and that of USA Gymnastics—some of the consequences of a discourse–materiality split and individualized agency are apparent. The discourse–materiality split allows individuals and organizations to overlook violence. For example, the assumption that words naturally correspond to the world allowed the judge to decide that a school need not respond to evidence of wrongdoing; after all, no one had used the phrase "sexual relationship" to describe the problematic behavior. Individualized agency similarly allows individuals and organizations to defer responses to violence. USA Gymnastics argued that only the person who experienced assault—or that person's parent—can file an actionable complaint. If other organizational members know about wrongdoing, the organization need not do anything. One outcome of these two problematic assumptions is that patterns of harm become difficult to notice. When an individual commits assaults against multiple individuals, and when a dominant group maintains the systems and structures that allow that group's violence to continue against a marginalized group, those components of violence escape attention. To combat these possible outcomes, organizations can implement processes that challenge representational accounts and individualized agency. I outline some specific ways for U.S. universities to do so in the next section.

How to move beyond the rapist: Advice for universities and other organizations

Given the arguments I have made, how can universities and other organizations move beyond the rapist? How can they implement some of the ideas developed in this book? I offer four suggestions.

First, whenever universities and other organizations publish information about sexual assault, they should situate it within the context of prevalence studies. So, for example, when colleges send out emergency alerts about sexual assault—per the requirements of the Clery Act—the message should include a minimum of one sentence about how many assaults happen nationally each year and the rate of sexual violence at U.S. universities. Other publications, such as annual safety statistics and campus climate survey results, should always include a summary of knowledge regarding rates of sexual violence among college students. Providing this information can help people to think beyond the rapist and to understand how an individual rape fits within a larger pattern of violence. Public health experts concur on this point: Situating any incident of gender-based violence within a larger framework builds the case for social transformation (Savage, Scarduzio, Harris, & Carlyle, 2017).

Second, researchers of sexual violence should continue to build knowledge about assault through multiple modalities. Narrative, arts-based, musical, danced, embodied, critical, and qualitative inquiries are all necessary to complement traditional prevalence studies. Because the traditional prevalence studies get caught in the representation trap that keeps a discourse–material divide intact and stalls transformation, people who wish to eradicate rape culture must continue to educate the public about sexual violence through multiple ways of knowing. Nuanced and rigorous knowledge includes the affective, emotional, abstract, and elusive aspects of trauma, ones that a representational mode fails to capture. Additionally, members of universities and other organizations should think broadly about how to evidence violence and should not focus only on counts of rapes and other assaults. In the case of higher education, those wishing to transform the culture might also pay attention to attrition rates that differ by gender/race/sexuality, mental illnesses that disproportionately affect members of marginalized university groups, educational discourses that deem students in dominant groups most valuable, and the underrepresentation of racial minorities in institutions of higher education. Each one of these phenomena tells part of the story of sexual violence and builds a framework that emphasizes violent organizational processes rather than discrete events.

Third, when presenting violence prevention programs, universities and other organizations should (a) situate any instance of rape or other sexual violence within larger social and cultural dynamics and (b) understand the relationship between what people say about rape and the behaviors of individuals who commit an instance of rape. To accomplish these aims, schools and other organizations could rely on frameworks developed among organizational communication scholars, ones that link micro-level, everyday conversation with macro-level, broad social meanings (e.g., Alvesson & Kärreman, 2000; Fairhurst, 2009). Elsewhere, I have written about how to integrate this type of thinking into sexual consent education so that prevention programs avoid the representationalist trap (K. L. Harris, 2018b). This framework encourages people to think beyond the rapist. For example, if a student in a prevention education program says of her friend who experienced sexual assault, "You know, she did go back to his place. That's kind of asking for it," then the educator can interrogate why and how being in a private space became equated with sexual availability. The student's interpretation is not unique: The comment invokes a long history in which vulnerable people—particularly women—are expected to be in domestic spaces only if they are performing a specific, sexual role. By always connecting everyday talk to repeated societal discourse, educators can encourage students not to get stuck debating the details of an individual instance of rape. Instead, they can encourage students—and other organizational members—to identify patterns in talk about rape and other sexual violence. Those patterns, as communication scholars have shown for other social phenomena, make some behaviors acceptable, normal, and even rewarded. By helping people to notice the influence of these broad societal discourses on everyday interactions—including statements and assaults—educators and organizational members can cultivate systemic thinking that enlarges the circle of concern beyond the rapist.

Finally, universities and other organizations should also offer trauma-informed trainings to their members. In higher education, students, faculty, and staff—especially those faculty and staff who investigate and adjudicate sexual assault—need this information. Education about how trauma affects memory can help those who have not experienced rape to understand its impacts. For a person who has experienced assault or other trauma, neurobiological processes—including the chemical states of the brain—shape how that person can provide accounts of the experience. Because they highlight the interactions between physiology and language use, trauma-informed trainings challenge the discourse–materiality bifurcation. Moreover, they help people who offer survivors support to understand what has happened. Instead of dismissing a friend as dishonest because that friend is unable to recall specific details of an assault, a college student who has received trauma-informed training may instead wonder whether the friend's memory lapse is a result of trauma. Likewise, an informed investigator may, rather than discount a rape complaint because the person's story shifts several times, understand that people who have experienced rape may have difficulty recounting what happened because trauma impacts memory and linear thinking.

Conclusion

In the introductory chapter, I suggested that one iteration of the violence–communication relationship operates in the realm of fantasy. Words and violence collapse upon one another such that a mere incantation can slice off an ear, as in J. K. Rowling's magical world. This position is not useful for addressing the problem of rape on U.S. campuses. Words alone do not commit sexual violence. The feminist new materialist approach I have outlined suggests that the human realm of discourse is not forceful by itself. Action is the sole purchase of neither symbols nor humans. Violence, then, emerges through constant intra-actions of material–discursive worlds that are always coming into being. At the outset of the book, I also pushed back against the children's ditty, "Sticks and stones can break my bones but words can never hurt me." The riddle proclaims the speaker's emotional toughness, and it nods to people's abilities to develop extraordinary psychological defenses against verbal abuse. Though it is useful to notice humans' power to resist mistreatment, it is not so useful to separate communication and violence completely, as this statement does. If injuries are only physical, then the connections between an utterance and the material–discursive configurations that precede and exceed it evaporate. Violence accumulates in those historical systems and structures—including words—that apportion and deny resources unequally and that negatively impact some people's bodies, mental health, economic security, and reproduction. Without challenging a bifurcation between throwing sticks and words, the organization of violence cannot come into view.

Keeping the organizational dimensions of sexual assault in view is essential in the contemporary social climate. As I was finishing revisions to this book, Title IX processes looked much different than when I started researching it. U.S. Secretary of Education Betsy DeVos announced changes to Title IX guidance in late 2017. Under her leadership, the Department of Education rescinded a number of its previously issued provisions. It eliminated the requirement that universities complete an investigation within 60 days and instead required a "good faith effort" to investigate in a "timely manner" (U.S. Department of Education, 2017, p. 3). It amended previous guidance so that schools could offer an appeal only to the respondent but not the complainant. And whereas previous guidance required schools to use "preponderance of evidence" as their standard of proof, the late 2017 changes allowed schools to choose between "preponderance of evidence" or the more stringent "clear and convincing" standard. Legal scholars and student conduct professionals, among others, pointed out that "preponderance of evidence" is used for all cases of discrimination and civil rights, including those under Title VI and Title VII of the Civil Rights Act of 1964 (e.g., Baker, Brake, & Cantalupo, 2016; Loschiavo & Waller, n.d.). To allow schools to use the "clear and convincing" standard means that claims of discrimination related to sexual assault would be held to a higher standard than any other type of discrimination, a difference that builds inequality into campuses' systems of redress.

By allowing schools more choice and flexibility, the Office for Civil Rights (OCR) appeared to become more neutral. But in cases of systemic trauma and violence, neutrality aligns organizations with perpetrators. Herman (1997) explained this well in her book on trauma:

> Those who bear witness [to trauma] are caught in the conflict between victim and perpetrator. It is morally impossible to remain neutral in this conflict. The bystander is forced to take sides. It is very tempting to take the side of the perpetrator. All the perpetrator asks is that the bystander do nothing. He appeals to the universal desire to see, hear, and speak no evil. The victim, on the contrary, asks the bystander to share the burden of pain. The victim demands action, engagement, and remembering. (pp. 7–8)

Though Herman's comments were aimed at psychological professionals, the same principle extends to the 2017 statements from the Department of Education. Giving schools more options for how they set up adjudication seems to make OCR more impartial. In reality, it means OCR will not admonish schools that, for example, allow an accused student to appeal a disciplinary measure but do not allow a student who makes a complaint of assault to do the same. On the whole, as I finished this book, the policymaking seemed to be newly driven by the myth that innocent people experience systematic false accusations and mistreatment. That notion simply does not square with vast evidence to the contrary. When organizational systems are complicit with domination, inaction amounts to support of the status quo and, therefore, a moral stance requires action and engagement aligned with those who have experienced sexual violence.

The outcome of an investigation concluded in 2017, conducted by OCR, illustrates the ongoing necessity of Title IX and its crucial role in a system that spurs organizational change. The outcome also illustrates the limitations and insufficiencies of Title IX processes in delivering justice for survivors. The case focused on Sarah Gilchriese, whom I met while she was an undergraduate student at the University of Colorado (CU) and who has identified herself in public media. One of Gilchriese's fellow students—whose name is not public knowledge—raped her in February 2013. After Gilchriese filed a complaint with the university, the school initiated an investigation. The university later found him in violation of the student code of conduct and deemed him responsible for what they called "non-consensual sexual intercourse," "non-consensual sexual contact," and "sexual harassment." The university disciplined the student by requiring him to pay a $75 fee, write a five- to seven-page essay, and have no contact with Gilchriese. They also suspended him for the remainder of the spring semester and the subsequent fall semester, after which time he would be allowed to return to the university. Under that timeline, the student who raped Gilchriese could return to campus while she was still enrolled in classes. After deciding on these sanctions and communicating them to the student and Gilchriese, it took the university a month to require the student to leave the campus. During that time, he approached Gilchriese on two separate occasions, despite the university's clear statement that he should not have any contact with her. When Gilchriese alerted the university of these contacts, the school did not take action to enforce its sanctions.

Concerned that the disciplinary measures were too light, implemented too slowly, and not fully enforced, Gilchriese filed a federal complaint with OCR, and she described that decision in her honors thesis (Gilchriese, 2015). That office began an investigation into whether CU was out of compliance with Title IX in its handling of her case. While the federal investigation was ongoing, CU hired Pepper Hamilton, a law firm, to conduct an independent, external investigation and advise the university about how to proceed. Per the recommendations resulting from that separate investigation, CU paid Gilchriese a monetary settlement. The university then also hired a new Title IX director and a coordinator for violence prevention programming, and it made other changes to improve its responses to sexual assault. Without Gilchriese's complaint, the federal and independent investigation that she spurred, and the media attention that resulted from her complaints, these changes and improvements in the university's processes would not have occurred. Even so, when the members of OCR concluded their investigation, they made no judgment about whether the university violated Title IX when it handled Gilchriese's case. They noted only that the university was in compliance with Title IX by the time they closed their investigation, more than four years after Gilchriese's initial complaint. Gilchriese summarized her thoughts on the process:

> After four-and-a-half years of my life filled with PTSD and anxiety from the rape itself, press surrounding my complaint, lawyers' meetings for restraining orders and my Title IX settlement, a 60-plus-page thesis outlining my experience at the University from an academic approach, and continually being contacted for papers, reports, and anything related to Title IX, it all came to an end with statements from the government that looked identical to the University webpage about the office handling assaults. . . . While I'm happy and proud that the University changed many policies, there is still work to be done. (Gilchriese, personal communication, October 11, 2017)

Gilchriese noted her appreciation for the workers who conduct these investigations but also expressed frustration with the university's response to OCR's findings. CU's press statements

144 | BEYOND THE RAPIST

implied that OCR found the university did nothing wrong, but the university cannot support that claim. It can only say that OCR now finds the school in compliance. Gilchriese said her initial goal was to improve the system at CU for other survivors, and she accomplished that. Even so, she remains without answers from OCR as to whether CU did, in fact, violate Title IX processes during 2013.

Gilchriese's case illustrates that Title IX is crucially important for prompting complex, multifaceted processes that push back on sexual violence and pressure organizations to do a better job of addressing rape. The law matters. Organizations, students, and employees need it for necessary transformations. Even so, the systemic changes required throughout organizations—and full justice—cannot be linked to Title IX alone. Institutions of higher education—and myriad other organizations—also need to shift their attention past individual instances of rape and other sexual violence to the patterns and processes that exist beyond the rapist.

References

Ahmed, S. (2008). Some preliminary remarks on the founding gestures of the "new materialism." *European Journal of Women's Studies, 15*, 23–39. doi:10.1177/1350506807084854

Alaimo, S. (2011). New materialisms, old humanisms, or following the submersible. *NORA: Nordic Journal of Feminist and Gender Research, 19*, 280–284. doi:10.1080/08038740.2011.618812

Alaimo, S., & Hekman, S. (Eds.). (2008). *Material feminisms.* Bloomington: Indiana University Press.

Alvesson, M., & Kärreman, D. (2000). Varieties of discourse: On the study of organizations through discourse analysis. *Human Relations, 53*, 1125–1149. doi:10.1177/0018726700539002

Alvesson, M., & Kärreman, D. (2011). Decolonizing discourse: Critical reflections on organizational discourse analysis. *Human Relations, 64*, 1121–1146. doi:10.1177/0018726711408629

Ashcraft, K. L., & Allen, B. J. (2003). The racial foundation of organizational communication. *Communication Theory, 13*, 5–38. doi:10.1111/j.1468-2885.2003.tb00280.x

Ashcraft, K. L., & Harris, K. L. (2014). "Meaning that matters": An organizational communication perspective on gender, discourse, and materiality. In S. Kumra, R. Simpson, & R. Burke (Eds.), *The Oxford handbook of gender in organizations* (pp. 130–150). New York, NY: Oxford University Press.

Baird, S., & Jenkins, S. R. (2003). Vicarious traumatization, secondary traumatic stress, and burnout in sexual assault and domestic violence agency staff. *Violence and Victims, 18*, 71–86. doi:10.1891/vivi.2003.18.1.71

Baker, K. K., Brake, D. L., & Cantalupo, N. C. (2016, August). Title IX & the preponderance of the evidence: A white paper. Retrieved from http://www.feministlawprofessors.com/wp-content/uploads/2016/08/Title-IX-Preponderance-White-Paper-signed-10.3.16.pdf

Barad, K. (1998). Getting real: Technoscientific practices and the materialization of reality. *Differences: A Journal of Feminist Cultural Studies, 10*(2), 87–128.

Barad, K. (2003). Posthumanist performativity: Toward an understanding of how matter comes to matter. *Signs: Journal of Women in Culture and Society, 28,* 803–831. doi:10.1086/345321

Barad, K. (2007). *Meeting the universe halfway: Quantum physics and the entanglement of matter and meaning.* Durham, NC: Duke University Press.

Barad, K. (2014). Diffracting diffraction: Cutting together apart. *Parallax, 20,* 168–187. doi:10.1080/13534645.2014.927623

Bartholet, E., Brewer, S., Donahue, C., Gertner, N., Halley, J., Hay, B. L., . . . Tribe, L. H. (2015, November 11). Press release re: *The Hunting Ground.* Retrieved from https://www.scribd.com/doc/289393251/Statement-on-Hunting-Ground

Becker, A. (2015a). *Newly released campus sexual violence data raise red flags.* Washington, DC: American Association of University Women. Retrieved from http://www.aauw.org/article/campus-sexual-violence-data/

Becker, A. (2015b). *Ninety-one percent of colleges reported zero incidents of rape in 2014.* Washington, DC: American Association of University Women. Retrieved from http://www.aauw.org/article/clery-act-data-analysis/

Bennett, J. (2005). The agency of assemblages and the North American blackout. *Public Culture, 17,* 445–465. doi:10.1215/08992363-17-3-445

Bergin, J., & Westwood, R. I. (2003). The necessities of violence. *Culture and Organization, 9,* 211–223. doi:10.1080/14759550420000195454

Bessant, J. (1998). Women in academia and opaque violence. *Melbourne Studies in Education, 39*(2), 41–67. doi:10.1080/17508489809556317

Birrell, P. J., & Freyd, J. J. (2006). Betrayal trauma: Relational models of harm and healing. *Journal of Trauma Practice, 5*(1), 49–63. doi:10.1300/J189v05n01_04

Braidotti, R. (2006). *Transpositions: On nomadic ethics*. Malden, MA: Polity.

Braidotti, R. (2010). The politics of "life itself" and new ways of dying. In D. Coole & S. Frost (Eds.), *New materialisms: Ontology, agency, and politics* (pp. 201–218). Durham, NC: Duke University Press.

Brewin, C. R. (2007). What is it that a neurobiological model of PTSD must explain? *Progress in Brain Research, 167*, 217–228. doi:10.1016/S0079-6123(07)67015-0

Broadfoot, K. J., & Munshi, D. (2015). Agency as a process of translation. *Management Communication Quarterly, 29*, 469–474. doi:10.1177/0893318915585158

Bruce, K., & Nyland, C. (2011). Elton Mayo and the deification of human relations. *Organization Studies, 32*, 383–405. doi:10.1177/0170840610397478

Brummans, B. H. J. M. (2007). Death by document: Tracing the agency of a text. *Qualitative Inquiry, 13*, 711–727. doi:10.1177/1077800407301185

Bumiller, K. (2008). *In an abusive state: How neoliberalism appropriated the feminist movement against sexual violence*. Durham, NC: Duke University Press.

Butler, J. (1993). *Bodies that matter: On the discursive limits of "sex."* New York, NY: Routledge.

Butler, J. (1997). *Excitable speech: A politics of the performative*. New York, NY: Routledge.

Caldwell, R. (2007). Agency and change: Re-evaluating Foucault's legacy. *Organization, 14*, 769–791. doi:10.1177/1350508407082262

Campbell, K. K. (2005). Agency: Promiscuous and protean. *Communication and Critical/Cultural Studies, 2*, 1–19. doi:10.1080/14791420042000332134

Campbell, R. (2002). *Emotionally involved: The impact of researching rape*. New York, NY: Routledge.

Campbell, R., & Raja, S. (1999). Secondary victimization of rape victims: Insights from mental health professionals who treat survivors of violence. *Violence and Victims, 14*, 261–275. doi:10.1891/0886-6708.14.3.261

Carey, J. W. (2009). *Communication as culture, revised edition: Essays on media and society*. New York, NY: Routledge.

Carillo Rowe, A. (2009). Subject to power: Feminism without victims. *Women's Studies in Communication, 32*, 12–35. doi:10.1080/07491409.2009.10162379

Carlile, P. R., Nicolini, D., Langley, A., & Tsoukas, H. (2013). *How matter matters: Objects, artifacts, and materiality in organization studies*. Oxford, United Kingdom: Oxford University Press.

Carrington, A. (2017). Mike Brown's body: New materialism and Black form. *ASAP/Journal, 2*, 276–283. doi:10.1353/asa.2017.0025

Caruth, C. (2014). *Listening to trauma: Conversations with leaders in the theory and treatment of catastrophic experience*. Baltimore, MD: Johns Hopkins University Press.

Catley, B. (2005). Workplace violence and the forging of management and organization history. *International Critical Management Studies Conference*, Cambridge, United Kingdom. Retrieved from http://www.mngt.waikato.ac.nz/ejrot/cmsconference/2005/proceedings/managementorganizational/Catley.pdf

Catley, B., & Jones, C. (2002). Deciding on violence. *Philosophy of Management, 2*(1), 25–34. doi:10.5840/pom20022120

Chakravartty, P., Kuo, R., Grubbs, V., & McIlwain, C. (2018). #CommunicationSoWhite. *Journal of Communication, 68*, 254–266. doi:10.1093/joc/jqy003

Chamberlain, L. J., Crowley, M., Tope, D., & Hodson, R. (2008). Sexual harassment in organizational context. *Work and Occupation, 35*, 262–295. doi:10.1177/0730888408322008

Cheah, P. (1996). Mattering. *Diacritics, 26*(1), 108–139. doi:10.1353/dia.1996.0004

Chen, C.-I., Dulani, J., & Piepzna-Samarasinha, L. (Eds.). (2016). *The revolution starts at home: Confronting intimate violence within activist communities*. Chico, CA: AK Press.

Cifor, M. (2016). Acting up, talking back: TITA, TIARA, and the value of gossip. *InterActions: UCLA Journal of Education and Information Studies, 12*(1). Retrieved from http://escholarship.org/uc/item/9d2007bj

Clair, R. P. (1993a). The bureaucratization, commodification, and privatization of sexual harassment through institutional discourse: A study of the Big Ten universities. *Management Communication Quarterly, 7*, 123–157. doi:10.1177/0893318993007002001

Clair, R. P. (1993b). The use of framing devices to sequester organizational narratives: Hegemony and harassment. *Communication Monographs, 60*, 113–136. doi:10.1080/03637759309376304

Clair, R. P. (1998). *Organizing silence: A world of possibilities*. Albany: State University of New York Press.

Clare, S. (2016). On the politics of "new feminist materialisms." In V. Pitts-Taylor (Ed.), *Mattering: Feminism, science, and materialism* (pp. 58–72). New York: New York University Press.

Conrad, C., & Taylor, B. (1994). The context(s) of sexual harassment: Power, silences, and academe. In S. G. Bingham (Ed.), *Conceptualizing sexual harassment as discursive practice* (pp. 45–58). Westport, CT: Praeger.

Coole, D., & Frost, S. (Eds.). (2010). *New materialisms: Ontology, agency, and politics.* Durham, NC: Duke University Press.

Cooper, M. M. (2011). Rhetorical agency as emergent and enacted. *College Composition and Communication, 62,* 420–449. Retrieved from http://www.ncte.org/library/NCTEFiles/Resources/Journals/CCC/0623-feb2011/CCC0623Rhetorical.pdf

Cooren, F. (2004). Textual agency: How texts do things in organizational settings. *Organization, 11,* 373–393. doi:10.1177/1350508404041998

Craig, R. T. (1999). Communication theory as a field. *Communication Theory, 9,* 119–161. doi:10.1111/j.1468-2885.1999.tb00355.x

Crenshaw, K. (1989). Demarginalizing the intersection of race and sex: A Black feminist critique of antidiscrimination doctrine, feminist theory and antiracist politics. *The University of Chicago Legal Forum,* 139–167.

Crenshaw, K. (1991). Mapping the margins: Intersectionality, identity politics, and violence against women of color. *Stanford Law Review, 43,* 1241–1299. doi:10.2307/1229039

Das, V. (2007). *Life and words: Violence and the descent into the ordinary.* Berkeley: University of California Press.

Davis, A. (2000). The color of violence against women. *ColorLines, 3*(3). Retrieved from http://colorlines.com/archives/2000/10/the_color_of_violence_against_women.html

Davis, N. (2009). New materialism and feminism's anti-biologism: A response to Sara Ahmed. *European Journal of Women's Studies, 16,* 67–80. doi:10.1177/1350506808098535

Delphy, C. (1977). *The main enemy: A materialist analysis of women's oppression.* London, England: Women's Research and Resource Centre.

Derlega, V. J., & Grzelak, J. (1979). Appropriateness of self-disclosure. In G. J. Chelune (Ed.), *Self-disclosure: Origins, patterns, and implications of openness in interpersonal relationships* (pp. 151–176). San Francisco, CA: Jossey-Bass.

Dolphijn, R., & van der Tuin, I. (2012). *New materialism: Interviews and cartographies*. Ann Arbor, MI: Open Humanities Press.

Dougherty, D. S., & Goldstein Hode, M. (2016). Binary logics and the discursive interpretation of organizational policy: Making meaning of sexual harassment policy. *Human Relations, 69*, 1729–1755. doi:10.1177/0018726715624956

Dougherty, D. S., & Smythe, M. J. (2004). Sensemaking, organizational culture, and sexual harassment. *Journal of Applied Communication Research, 32*, 293–317. doi:10.1080/0090988042000275998

Eisenberg, E. M., & Witten, M. G. (1987). Reconsidering openness in organizational communication. *The Academy of Management Review, 12*, 418–426. doi:10.5465/AMR.1987.4306557

Enck-Wanzer, S. M. (2009). All's fair in love and sport: Black masculinity and domestic violence in the news. *Communication and Critical/Cultural Studies, 6*, 1–18. doi:10.1080/14791420802632087

Fackler, M. F. (2010). "I'll google it": Gossip, queer intimacies, and the Internet. *Modern Drama, 53*, 390–409. doi:10.3138/md.53.3.390

Faculty Against Rape. (2016, April 15). FAR AAUP Title IX letter. Retrieved from https://docs.google.com/document/d/1yXsrWoV GqN725vepBZfemKuhbUzbgYiMo0ruX38qJJY/edit

Fairhurst, G. T. (2009). Considering context in discursive leadership research. *Human Relations, 62*, 1607–1633. doi:10.1177/0018726709346379

Fannin, M., MacLeavy, J., Larner, W., & Wang, W. W. (2014). Work, life, bodies: New materialisms and feminisms. *Feminist Theory, 15*, 261–268. doi:10.1177/1464700114545320

Figley, C. R. (Ed.). (1995). *Compassion fatigue: Coping with secondary traumatic stress disorder in those who treat the traumatized*. New York, NY: Brunner Mazel.

Fisher, B. S. (2009). The effects of survey question wording on rape estimates: Evidence from a quasi-experimental design. *Violence Against Women, 15*, 133–147. doi:10.1177/1077801208329391

Fleetwood, S. (2005). Ontology in organization and management studies: A critical realist perspective. *Organization, 12*, 192–222. doi:10.1177/1350508405051188

Franklin v. Gwinnet County Public Schools, 503 U.S. 60 (1992).

Fraser, M. (2002). What is the matter of feminist criticism. *Economy and Society, 31*, 606–625. doi:10.1080/03085140022000020715

Frost, S. (2011). The implications of new materialisms for feminist epistemology. In H. E. Grasswick (Ed.), *Feminist epistemology and philosophy of science: Power in knowledge* (pp. 69–83). New York, NY: Springer.

Geertz, E., & van der Tuin, I. (2013). From intersectionality to interference: Feminist onto-epistemological reflections on the politics of representation. *Women's Studies International Forum, 41,* 171–178. doi:10.1016/j.wsif.2013.07.013

Gerencser, S. (2005). The corporate person and democratic politics. *Political Research Quarterly, 58,* 625–635. doi:10.1177/106591290505800410

Gilchriese, S. (2015). *Organizational discourse and discursive closure on college sex assaults: An autoethnography about filing a Title IX complaint* (Unpublished undergraduate honors thesis). University of Colorado, Boulder, CO. Retrieved from http://scholar.colorado.edu/honr_theses/926/

Grosz, E. (1994). *Volatile bodies: Toward a corporeal feminism.* Bloomington: Indiana University Press.

Grosz, E. (2010). The untimeliness of feminist theory. *NORA: Nordic Journal of Feminist and Gender Research, 18,* 48–51. doi:10.1080/08038741003627039

Grosz, E. (2017). *The incorporeal: Ontology, ethics, and the limits of materialism.* New York, NY: Columbia University Press.

Haag, P. (1996). "Putting your body on the line": The question of violence, victims, and the legacies of second-wave feminism. *Differences: A Journal of Feminist Cultural Studies, 8*(2), 23–67.

Haag, P. (1999). *Consent: Sexual rights and the transformation of American liberalism.* Ithaca, NY: Cornell University Press.

Hallenbeck, S. (2012). Toward a posthuman perspective: Feminist rhetorical methodologies and everyday practices. *Advances in the History of Rhetoric, 15,* 9–27. doi:10.1080/15362426.2012.657044

Hamby, S. L., & Koss, M. P. (2003). Shades of gray: A qualitative study of terms used in the measurement of sexual victimization. *Psychology of Women Quarterly, 27,* 243–255. doi:10.1111/1471-6402.00104

Haraway, D. (1992). The promises of monsters: A regenerative politics for inappropriate/d others. In L. Grossberg, C. Nelson, & P. Treichler (Eds.), *Cultural studies* (pp. 296–337). New York, NY: Routledge.

Haraway, D. (1997). *Second_Millennium.FemaleMan©_Meets_OncoMouse™: Feminism and Technoscience.* New York, NY: Routledge.

Harding, S. (1995). "Strong objectivity": A response to the new objectivity question. *Synthese, 104,* 331–349. doi:10.1007/bf01064504

Hardy, C., Phillips, N., & Clegg, S. (2001). Reflexivity in organization and management theory: A study of the production of the research "'subject'." *Human Relations, 54,* 531–560. doi:10.1177/0018726701545001

Harris, C. I. (1993). Whiteness as property. *Harvard Law Review, 1066,* 1707–1791. doi:10.2307/1341787

Harris, K. L. (2011). The next problem with no name: The politics and pragmatics of the word *rape. Women's Studies in Communication, 34,* 42–63. doi:10.1080/07491409.2011.566533

Harris, K. L. (2013). Show them a good time: Organizing the intersections of sexual violence. *Management Communication Quarterly, 27,* 568–595. doi:10.1177/0893318913506519

Harris, K. L. (2016a). Feminist dilemmatic theorizing: New materialism in communication studies. *Communication Theory, 26,* 103–211. doi:10.1111/comt.12083

Harris, K. L. (2016b). Reflexive voicing: A communicative approach to intersectional writing. *Qualitative Research, 16,* 111–127. doi:10.1177/1468794115569560

Harris, K. L. (2017). Re-situating organizational knowledge: Violence, intersectionality, and the privilege of partial perspective. *Human Relations, 70,* 263–285. doi:10.1177/0018726716654745

Harris, K. L. (2018a). Mapping gender and violence: Describing reality, resisting abuse. *Women's Studies in Communication, 41,* 113–116. doi:10.1080/07491409.2018.1463770

Harris, K. L. (2018b). Yes means yes and no means no, but both these mantras need to go: Communication myths in consent education and anti-rape activism. *Journal of Applied Communication Research, 46,* 155–178. doi:10.1080/00909882.2018.1435900

Harris, K. L., & Fortney, J. M. (2017). Reflexive caring: Rethinking reflexivity through trauma and disability. *Text and Performance Quarterly, 37,* 20–34. doi:10.1080/10462937.2016.1273543

Harris, K. L., & Hanchey, J. N. (2014). (De)stabilizing sexual violence discourse: Masculinization of victimhood, organizational blame, and labile imperialism. *Communication and Critical/Cultural Studies, 11,* 322–341. doi:10.1080/14791420.2014.972421

Hartsock, N. C. M. (1983). The feminist standpoint: Developing the ground for a specifically feminist historical materialism. In S. Harding & M. B. Hintikka (Eds.), *Discovering reality: Feminist perspectives on epistemology, metaphysics, methodology, and philosophy of science* (pp. 283–310). Dordrecht, Holland: Kluwer Academic.

Harvard Law Administrative Board. (2011). Report of the Administrative Board Hearing of September 19, 2011. Retrieved from http://www.thehuntinggroundfilm.com/wp-content/uploads/2015/10/ReportoftheAdministrativeBoardHearingofSeptember192011-Kamilah.pdf

Hassard, J. S. (2012). Rethinking the Hawthorne Studies: The Western Electric research in its social, political and historical context. *Human Relations, 65,* 1431–1461. doi:10.1177/0018726712452168

Hearn, J. (1998). *The violences of men: How men talk about and how agencies respond to men's violence to women.* Thousand Oaks, CA: Sage.

Hearn, J. (2003). Organization violations in practice: A case study in a university setting. *Culture and Organization, 9,* 253–273. doi:10.1080/1475955042000195436

Hearn, J., & Parkin, W. (2001). *Gender, sexuality and violence in organizations: The unspoken forces of organization violations.* Thousand Oaks, CA: Sage.

Hekman, S. (2009). Constructing the ballast: An ontology for feminism. In S. Alaimo & S. Hekman (Eds.), *Material feminisms* (pp. 85–119). Bloomington: Indiana University Press.

Hengehold, L. (2000). Remapping the event: Institutional discourses and the trauma of rape. *Signs: Journal of Women in Culture and Society, 26,* 189–214. doi:10.1086/495571

Herman, J. (1997). *Trauma and recovery: The aftermath of violence—from domestic violence to political terror.* New York, NY: Basic Books.

Hill, C. (2011). *Crossing the line: Sexual harassment at school.* Washington, DC: American Association of University Women. Retrieved from http://www.aauw.org/research/crossing-the-line/

Hinton, P., & van der Tuin, I. (2014). Preface. *Women: A Cultural Review, 25,* 1–8. doi:10.1080/09574042.2014.903781

Hird, M. J. (2004). Feminist matters: New materialist considerations of sexual difference. *Feminist Theory, 5,* 223–232. doi:10.1177/1464700104045411

Holmes, K. (2015). What's the tea: Gossip and the production of black gay social history. *Radical History Review*, *2015*(122), 55–69. doi:10.1215/01636545-2849531

Hope, A., & Eriksen, M. (2009). From military sexual trauma to "organization-trauma": Practising "poetics of testimony." *Culture and Organization*, *15*, 109–127. doi:10.1080/14759550802709582

How a perpetrator gets away with sexual harassment at CU Boulder [Blog post]. (2013, August 17). Retrieved from https://scientificfemanomaly.com/tag/sexual-assault/

INCITE! Women of Color Against Violence (Eds.). (2016). *Color of violence: The INCITE! anthology*. Durham, NC: Duke University Press.

Irni, S. (2013). The politics of materiality: Affective encounters in a transdisciplinary debate. *European Journal of Women's Studies*, *20*, 347–360. doi:10.1177/1350506812472669

Jackson, Z. I. (2013). Animal: New directions in the theorization of race and posthumanism. *Feminist Studies*, *39*, 669–685.

Jagger, G. (2015). The new materialism and sexual difference. *Signs: Journal of Women in Culture and Society*, *40*, 321–342. doi:10.1086/678190

Jenkins, M. A., Langlais, P. J., Delis, D., & Cohen, R. (1998). Learning and memory in rape victims with posttraumatic stress disorder. *American Journal of Psychiatry*, *155*, 278–279. doi:10.1176/ajp.155.2.278

Kaiser, B. M., & Thiele, K. (2014). Diffraction: Onto-epistemology, quantum physics and the critical humanities. *Parallax*, *20*, 165–167. doi:10.1080/13534645.2014.927621

Kendall, F. E. (2013). *Understanding white privilege: Creating pathways to authentic relationships across race* (2nd ed.). New York, NY: Routledge.

Kirby, V. (1997). *Telling flesh: The substance of the corporeal*. New York, NY: Routledge.

Koss, M. P., Abbey, A., Campbell, R., Cook, S., Norris, J., Testa, M., . . . White, J. (2007). Revising the SES: A collaborative process to improve assessment of sexual aggression and victimization. *Psychology of Women Quarterly*, *31*, 357–370. doi:10.1111/j.1471-6402.2007.00385.x

Kuznick, L., & Ryan, M. (2008). Changing norms? Title IX and legal activism. *Harvard Journal of Law & Gender*, *31*, 367–422. Retrieved from http://harvardjlg.com/wp-content/uploads/2012/01/367-377.pdf

Kwiatkowski, M., & Evans, T. (2016, August 26). Ex-gymnast speaks out about her sexual abuse. *The Indianapolis Star*. Retrieved from http://www.indystar.com/story/news/investigations/2016/08/26/kid-they-said-wasnt-worth/89339532/

Latour, B. (2004). Why has critique run out of steam?: From matters of fact to matters of concern. *Critical Inquiry, 30*, 225–248. doi:10.1086/421123

Lawrence, C. R., Matsuda, M. J., Delgado, R., & Crenshaw, K. W. (1993). Introduction. In M. Matsuda, C. R. Lawrence, R. Delgado, & K. W. Crenshaw (Eds.), *Words that wound: Critical race theory, assaultive speech, and the First Amendment* (pp. 1–15). Boulder, CO: Westview Press.

Leonardi, P. M. (2013). Theoretical foundations for the study of sociomateriality. *Information and Organization, 23*, 59–76. doi:10.1016/j.infoandorg.2013.02.002

Lieberwitz, R. L., Jaleel, R., Kelleher, T., Scott, J. W., Young, D., Runyan, A. S., . . . Levy, A. (2016). *The history, uses, and abuses of Title IX*. Washington, DC: American Association of University Professors. Retrieved from https://www.aaup.org/file/TitleIXreport.pdf

Lombardi, K., & Jones, K. (2009). *Campus sexual assault statistics don't add up: The troubling discrepancies in Clery Act numbers*. Washington, DC: The Center for Public Integrity. Retrieved from https://publicintegrity.org/education/sexual-assault-on-campus/campus-sexual-assault-statistics-dont-add-up/

Lonsway, K. A., Archambault, J., & Lisak, D. (2009). False reports: Moving beyond the issue to successfully investigate and prosecute non-stranger sexual assault. *The Voice, 3*(1), 1–11. Retrieved from https://www.nsvrc.org/sites/default/files/publications/2018-10/Lisak-False-Reports-Moving-beyond.pdf

Loschiavo, C., & Waller, J. L. (n.d.). *The preponderance of evidence standard: Use in higher education campus conduct processes*. Washington, DC: Association for Student Conduct Administration. Retrieved from http://www.theasca.org/files/The%20Preponderance%20of%20Evidence%20Standard.pdf

Lutgen-Sandvik, P., & Tracy, S. J. (2011). Answering five key questions about workplace bullying: How communication scholarship provides thought leadership for transforming abuse at work. *Management Communication Quarterly, 26*, 3–47. doi:10.1177/0893318911414400

MacKinnon, C. (2016). In their hands: Restoring institutional liability for sexual harassment in education. *Yale Law Journal, 125*, 2038–2105. Retrieved from http://www.yalelawjournal.org/feature/in-their-hands-restoring-institutional-liability-for-sexual-harassment-in-education

MacKinnon, C. A. (1989). *Toward a feminist theory of the state.* Cambridge, MA: Harvard University Press.

Malmsheimer, T. (2014, June 27). Conservatives are obsessed with debunking the 1-in-5 rape statistic. They're wrong, too. *New Republic.* Retrieved from http://www.newrepublic.com/article/118430/independent-womens-forum-challenges-one-five-statistic

Matthews, G., & Goodman, S. (Eds.). (2013). *Violence and the limits of representation.* New York, NY: Palgrave Macmillan.

May, S. K., Cheney, G., & Roper, J. (Eds.). (2007). *The debate over corporate social responsibility.* New York, NY: Oxford University Press.

McCall, L. (2001). *Complex inequality: Gender, class, and race in the new economy.* New York, NY: Routledge.

McCall, L. (2005). The complexity of intersectionality. *Signs: Journal of Women in Culture and Society, 30*, 1771–1800. doi:10.1086/426800

Messer-Davidow, E. (2002). *Disciplining feminism: From social activism to academic discourse.* Durham, NC: Duke University Press.

Meyers, E. A. (2015). Women, gossip, and celebrity online: Celebrity gossip blogs as feminized popular culture. In E. Levine (Ed.), *Cupcakes, Pinterest, and ladyporn: Feminized popular culture in the early twenty-first century* (pp. 71–94). Urbana: University of Illinois Press.

Milne-Smith, A. (2009). Club talk: Gossip, masculinity, and oral communities in late nineteenth-century London. *Gender & History, 21*, 86–106. doi:10.1111/j.1468-0424.2009.01536.x

Minh-ha, T. T. (1989). *Woman, native, other: Writing, postcoloniality, and feminism.* Bloomington: Indiana University Press.

Mohanty, C. T. (2003). Privatized citizenship, corporate academies, and feminist projects. In *Feminism without borders: Decolonizing theory, practicing solidarity* (pp. 169–189). Durham, NC: Duke University Press.

Muñoz, J. E., Haritaworn, J., Hird, M., Jackson, Z. I., Puar, J. K., Joy, E., . . . Halberstam, J. (2015). Dossier: Theorizing queer inhumanisms. *GLQ: A Journal of Lesbian and Gay Studies, 21*, 209–248. doi:10.1215/10642684-2843323

Mutch, A. (2013). Sociomateriality—Taking the wrong turning? *Information and Organization*, *23*, 28–40. doi:10.1016/j.infoandorg.2013.02.001

National Center for Education Statistics. (n.d.). *Fast facts: Enrollment*. Washington, DC: Institute of Education Sciences. Retrieved from https://nces.ed.gov/FastFacts/display.asp?id=98

New, J. (2015, May 6). Justice delayed. *Inside Higher Ed*. Retrieved from https://www.insidehighered.com/news/2015/05/06/ocr-letter-says-completed-title-ix-investigations-2014-lasted-more-4-years

Nkomo, S. M. (1992). The emperor has no clothes: Rewriting "race in organizations." *Academy of Management Review*, *17*, 487–513. doi:10.5465/AMR.1992.4281987

Office on Violence Against Women. (2016). *Frequently asked questions: Campus climate surveys*. Washington, DC: U.S. Department of Justice. Retrieved from https://www.justice.gov/ovw/file/902106/download

Office on Violence Against Women. (2017, January 8). *Protecting students from sexual assault*. Washington, DC: U.S. Department of Justice. Retrieved from https://www.justice.gov/ovw/protecting-students-sexual-assault

Orchowski, L. M., & Gidycz, C. A. (2015). Psychological consequences associated with positive and negative responses to disclosure of sexual assault among college women: A prospective study. *Violence Against Women*, *21*, 803–823. doi:10.1177/1077801215584068

Orchowski, L. M., Untied, A. S., & Gidycz, C. A. (2013). Factors associated with college women's labeling of sexual victimization. *Violence and Victims*, *28*, 940–958. doi:10.1891/0886-6708.VV-D-12-00049

Pelzer, P. (2003). The dinner party of silent gentlemen: The intrinsic violence of organisations. *Culture and Organization*, *9*, 225–237. doi:10.1080/1475955042000195445

Potter, S. J., & Edwards, K. M. (2015). *Institutional Title IX requirements for researchers conducting human subjects research on sexual violence and other forms of interpersonal violence*. Durham, NH: Prevention Innovations Research Center. Retrieved from https://cola.unh.edu/sites/cola.unh.edu/files/departments/Prevention%20Innovations%20Research%20Center/pdf/Prevention_Innovations_Research_Center_Title_IX_Human_Subject_Research_White_Paper_Nov_5_2015docx.pdf

Raine, N. V. (1998). *After silence: Rape and my journey back*. New York, NY: Three Rivers Press.

Reed, M. (2000). The limits of discourse analysis in organizational analysis. *Organization, 7*, 524–530. doi:10.1177/135050840073011

Reed, M. (2005). Reflections on the realist turn in organization and management studies. *Journal of Management Studies, 42*, 1621–1644. doi:10.1111/j.1467-6486.2005.00559.x

Ricoeur, P. (1998). Violence and language. *Bulletin de la Société Américaine de Philosophie de Langue Française, 10*(2), 32–41. Retrieved from http://www.jffp.org/ojs/index.php/jffp/article/view/410/404

Robichaud, D., & Cooren, F. (Eds.). (2013). *Organization and organizing: Materiality, agency, and discourse*. New York, NY: Routledge.

Ryan, C. L., & Bauman, K. (2016, March). *Educational attainment in the United States: 2015 population characteristics*. Washington, DC: U.S. Census Bureau. Retrieved from https://www.census.gov/content/dam/Census/library/publications/2016/demo/p20-578.pdf

Salin, D. (2003). Ways of explaining workplace bullying: A review of enabling, motivating, and precipitating structures and processes in the work environment. *Human Relations, 56*, 1213–1232. doi:10.1177/00187267035610003

Samuelson, K. W. (2011). Post-traumatic stress disorder and declarative memory functioning: A review. *Dialogues in Clinical Neuroscience, 13*, 346–351.

Savage, M. W., Scarduzio, J. A., Harris, K. L., & Carlyle, K. E., & Sheff, S. E. (2017). News stories of intimate partner violence: An experimental examination of perpetrator sex and violence severity on seriousness, sympathy, and punishment preferences. *Health Communication, 32*, 768–776. doi:10.1080/10410236.2016.1217453

Scarry, E. (1985). *The body in pain: The making and unmaking of the world*. New York, NY: Oxford University Press.

Schauben, L. J., & Frazier, P. A. (1995). Vicarious trauma: The effects on female counselors of working with sexual violence survivors. *Psychology of Women Quarterly, 19*, 49–64. doi:10.1111/j.1471-6402.1995.tb00278.x

Schow, A. (2014, August 13). No, 1 in 5 women have not been raped on campus. *The Washington Examiner*. Retrieved from https://www.washingtonexaminer.com/no-1-in-5-women-have-not-been-raped-on-college-campuses

Scott, J. W. (1997). *Only paradoxes to offer: French feminists and the rights of man*. Cambridge, MA: Harvard University Press.

Sehgal, M. (2014). Diffractive propositions: Reading Alfred North Whitehead with Donna Haraway and Karen Barad. *Parallax, 20*, 188–201. doi:10.1080/13534645.2014.927625

Seshadri, K. R. (2012). *HumAnimal: Race, law, language*. Minneapolis: University of Minnesota Press.

Simpson v. University of Colorado, 372 F. Supp. 2d 1229 (District Court, D. Colorado 2005).

Simpson v. University of Colorado, 500 F. 3d 1170 (10th Cir. 2007).

Smith, A. (2005). *Conquest: Sexual violence and American Indian genocide*. Cambridge, MA: South End Press.

Sokoloff, N. J., & Pratt, C. (Eds.). (2005). *Domestic violence at the margins: Readings on race, class, gender, and culture*. New Brunswick, NJ: Rutgers University Press.

Sokolow, B. A. (n.d.). *A circuit split on Title IX?* Berwyn, PA: National Center for Higher Education Risk Management. Retrieved from https://www.ncherm.org/pdfs/CIRCUIT_SPLIT_TITLE_IX.pdf

Spacks, P. M. (1982). In praise of gossip. *The Hudson Review, 35*, 19–38. doi:10.2307/3851309

Spade, D. (2011). *Normal life: Administrative violence, critical trans politics, and the limits of law*. Brooklyn, NY: South End Press.

Spall, S. (1998). Peer debriefing in qualitative research: Emerging operational models. *Qualitative Inquiry, 4*, 280–292. doi:10.1177/107780049800400208

Starzynski, L. L., Ullman, S. E., Filipas, H. H., & Townsend, S. M. (2005). Correlates of women's sexual assault disclosure to informal and formal support sources. *Violence and Victims, 20*, 417–432. doi:10.1891/0886-6708.20.4.417

Stephens, E. (2014). Feminism and new materialism: The matter of fluidity. *InterAlia: A Journal of Queer Studies, 9*, 186–202. Retrieved from http://interalia.org.pl/media/09_2014/InterAlia_9_2014_Bodily_Fluids.pdf

Tannen, D. (2001). *You just don't understand: Women and men in conversation*. New York, NY: Quill.

Thimsen, A. F. (2015). The people against corporate personhood: *Doxa* and dissensual democracy. *Quarterly Journal of Speech, 101*, 485–508. doi:10.1080/00335630.2015.1055785

Title IX of the Education Amendments of 1972, 20 U.S.C. §§ 1681–1688.

Todd, Z. (2016). An indigenous feminist's take on the ontological turn: "Ontology" is just another word for colonialism. *Journal of Historical Sociology, 29,* 4–22. doi:10.1111/johs.12124

Tompkins, P. K., & Wanca-Thibault, M. (2001). Organizational communication: Prelude and prospects. In F. M. Jablin & L. L. Putnam (Eds.), *The new handbook of organizational communication: Advances in theory, research, and methods* (pp. xvii–xxxi). Thousand Oaks, CA: Sage.

U.S. Army. (2012). *Army 2020: Generating health and discipline in the force ahead of the strategic reset.* Washington, DC: Department of the Army. Retrieved from http://preventsuicide.army.mil/docs/Army_2020_Generating_Health_and_Discipline_in_the_Force_Report_2012_GOLD_BOOK.pdf

U.S. Department of Education. (2017, September). *Q&A on campus sexual misconduct.* Washington, DC: Office for Civil Rights. Retrieved from https://www2.ed.gov/about/offices/list/ocr/docs/qa-title-ix-201709.pdf?utm_content=&utm_medium=email&utm_name=&utm_source=govdelivery&utm_term=

van der Tuin, I. (2009). "Jumping generations": On second- and third-wave feminist epistemology. *Australian Feminist Studies, 24,* 17–31. doi:10.1080/08164640802645166

van der Tuin, I. (2011). New feminist materialisms. *Women's Studies International Forum, 34,* 271–277. doi:10.1016/j.wsif.2011.04.002.

van der Tuin, I., & Dolphijn, R. (2010). The transversality of new materialism. *Women: A Cultural Review, 21,* 153–171. doi:10.1080/09574042.2010.488377

Violanti, M. T. (1996). Hooked on expectations: An analysis of influence and relationships in the Tailhook Reports. *Journal of Applied Communication Research, 24,* 67–82. doi:10.1080/00909889609365442

Westwood, R. I. (2003). Economies of violence: An autobiographical account. *Culture and Organization, 9,* 275–293. doi:10.1080/1475955042000195418

Wiegman, R. (1995). *American anatomies: Theorizing race and gender.* Durham, NC: Duke University Press.

Will, G. F. (2014, June 6). Colleges become the victims of progressivism. *The Washington Post.* Retrieved from http://www.washingtonpost.com/opinions/george-will-college-becomethe-victims-of-progressivism/2014/06/06/e90e73b4-eb50-11e3-9f5c-9075d5508f0a_story.html

Willingham, K. (2016, April 2). To the Harvard Law 19: Do better. *The Harvard Law Record*. Retrieved from http://hlrecord.org/2016/04/to-the-harvard-law-19-do-better/

Wood, J. T. (2013). *Gendered lives: Communication, gender, and culture* (10th ed.). Boston, MA: Wadsworth.

Žižek, S. (2008). *Violence: Six sideways reflections*. New York, NY: Picador.

Index